WHAT PEOP

Death to Selfie is a book that is needed in today's self-centered culture. We live in a world that is increasingly focused on the individual more than the corporate. In *Death to Selfie*, Will Owen takes the reader on a journey to the roots of how selfishness manifests and presents a roadmap that will lead to freedom. Will writes with both biblical precepts and the praxis of how to rid ourselves of selfishness and live selflessly. This book is a fantastic tool for today and will lead many to freedom and liberty.—JOSHUA GAY, PASTOR, HIGH PRAISE PANAMA CITY, PANAMA CITY FL

In Will Owen's book, *Death to Selfie*, he exposes the traps that the devil uses to ensnare people. There are not any new tactics or schemes which the enemy uses, it is the same doorways of the flesh that become the pathways for him to build his strongholds. Believers must fortify themselves from the assault of satan, which begins with closing all the openings that the fleshly and carnal man affords. This book will give the reader the keys needed to lock these doors and deal a death blow to the works of the flesh.—ROBERT GAY, PASTOR OF HIGH PRAISE PANAMA CITY, PANAMA CITY FL

Death to Selfie is an amazing book that has outlined destructive forces in the arena of the flesh and provokes you to look introspectively leading you to victory that comes solely through the blood of Christ!—RICARDO BETANCOURT, PRESIDENT OF SHALAM CONSTRUCTION, PANAMA CITY FL

In his book, *The City of God*, Saint Augustine of Hippo writes, "Pride is the beginning of sin. And what is pride but the craving of undue exaltation? And this is undue exaltation—when the soul abandons Him to whom it ought to cleave as its end, and becomes a kind of end to itself." In our overtly self(ie)-absorbed world, I cannot think of a more succinct diagnosis of the decay that is eating at us as humans and as a society. And that is why Will Owen's book has arrived just in time, carrying with it the only prescription that can truly heal us: death. It might seem paradoxical to suggest that death somehow generates new life, but that is precisely what Scripture affirms, and it is the same truth that *Death to Selfie* calls us back to. In a world rife with voices championing humans to "find themselves," Will suggests just the opposite: only in losing yourself to a life of following Jesus to the cross are you really, actually found.—CASEY DOSS, THE RAMP SCHOOL OF MINISTRY, HAMILTON AL

I am thrilled that this book has been written. Few books have been written that ministers to me so personally and have impacted me as a believer so profoundly as this one. *Death to Selfie* puts "self" in the right perspective and outlines the destructive forces of the "flesh" without the Holy Spirit. It causes us to look inward at our own self and account for the true motives of our heart. Are they dictating a life of sin and justification or a life of victory and fruitfulness? May this book find its way to the five-fold ministry, families, businessmen, and those who need it, and those who have been held captive to works of selfishness. This is truly a road map for youths and parents, employees and CEOs, businesses and churches, and needs to be widely read.—WILLIE MORRIS, INSTRUCTIONAL SYSTEMS DESIGNER-APPLIED RESEARCH ASSOCIATES, INC., PANAMA CITY FL

An extraordinarily timely and powerful book, *Death to Selfie* immerses the reader in the plans God has for each of us. It confronts the reader's notions of "mankind's sin nature" and focuses on the root of the issue itself: man's single-sided self-nature. Owen's book is deeply rooted in Scripture and presents God's Word in a way that will resonate with many. It allows the reader to be challenged with issues without bringing shame or judgment. Several times I felt challenged and realized I had work to do in my own life. Bringing his unique perspective on a case study of satan was enlightening. This is not just another self-help book. Indeed, it is a clarion call for each of us to strive to be more than we are now and move toward the high calling of Christ. In today's divisive culture, *Death to Selfie* is a book all Christians would benefit from reading and applying the principles presented within it. I highly recommend Owen's book.—DR. JAMIE BIRDWELL, EXECUTIVE VICE-PRESIDENT OF COAST, A LAURCON COMPANY, PANAMA CITY FL

DEATH TO SELFIE

WILL OWEN

DEATH TO SELFIE

A ROADMAP FOR CHRISTLIKE LIVING

Melbourne, Florida USA

Death to Selfie—A Roadmap for Christlike Living
by Will Owen

Parsons Publishing House
P. O. Box 410063
Melbourne
FL 32940 USA

www.ParsonsPublishingHouse.com
Info@ParsonsPublishingHouse.com

All Scripture quotations, unless otherwise indicated, are taken from the New King James Version, Thomas Nelson Publishers, Nashville: Thomas Nelson Publishers, Copyright 1982. Used by permission. All rights reserved.

Scripture quotations marked (MSG) are taken from THE MESSAGE, copyright © 1993, 1994, 1995, 1996, 2000, 2001, 2002 by Eugene H. Peterson. Used by permission of Nav Press. All rights reserved. Represented by Tyndale House Publishers, Inc.

Scripture quotations marked (NIV) are taken from the Holy Bible, New International Version®, NIV®. Copyright © 1973, 1978, 1984 by Biblica, Inc.TM Used by permission of Zondervan. All rights reserved worldwide. www.zondervan.com.

Scripture quotations marked (NLT) are taken from the Holy Bible, New Living Translation, copyright 1996, 2004, 2015. Used by permission of Tyndale House Publishers, Inc., Carol Stream, Illinois 60188. All rights reserved.

Publisher's Note: Disregarding English grammar rules, Publisher has opted to reference satan and related names with lowercase letters.

Front Cover Art: Micah Gay

Copyright © 2023 by Will Owen.
All rights reserved.
ISBN-13: 978-160273-151-6
ISBN-10: 160273151-9
Printed in the United States of America.
For World-Wide Distribution.

DEDICATION

To my wife Jennifer and children, Caleb, Barrett & Faith. You've motivated me to seek to be a better husband, father, and spiritual leader within our home. Through the process of writing this book, I have learned to walk out the teachings found within its pages. Thank you for your patience these 12 years as the Lord has done this work in me. Without having each of you in my life, this book would not have become a reality. I love each of you.

To Dr. Robert Gay, my spiritual covering and spiritual father. Thank you for believing in me and for pouring into me. Your willingness to pour into my life with both your time and wisdom has shaped much of who I am today. Much of what is written in this text was inspired by messages you preached on Sunday and Wednesday services. You truly sowed the seeds of this harvest.

DEATH TO SELFIE

FOREWORD
by Dr. Robert Gay

Looking honestly at the shape of today's culture and society, we can easily deduce and conclude that we live in a self-centered world. A brief scroll through social media platforms and forums reveals that people love to talk about themselves. A great number of the pictures posted on various pages are what have been called "selfies." They are quick and easy to take and just as easy to post, which allows the world to peek into the things involving our personal lives. The bottom line is that we live in a world consumed with self. This is not to say that a selfie is wrong or improper to post. These things just reveal the level of self-absorption that is common in our world today. The practice of these things, unchecked and to an extreme, has caused many people to become obsessed with themselves and opened the door for undesirable things.

When "self" is at the helm of anyone's ship, it is sure to evolve into fleshly and carnal expressions in their lives. Understand that what is meant by "self" is not you as an individual. The "self" I refer to is what the Bible calls the flesh. It is the carnal appetites and unrenewed mind present within people that provoke them to do things that are sinful

DEATH TO SELFIE

and destructive. It is the "selfishness" that the Bible specifically refers to as sin. When self is enthroned in anyone's life, it can produce disastrous effects.

The apostle John said that the world is filled with three things: the lust of the flesh, the lust of the eye, and the pride of life. All sinful activity can be broken down into one of these three categories. These doors enable satan to enter a person's life and provoke them to sin. There is no new methodology that the devil is using. It is the same thing he has used throughout the course of history. At the beginning of creation, Eve was tempted through all three of these doorways. The Bible declares that she saw (the lust of the eye) that the tree was desirable to eat (lust of the flesh) and a tree to make one wise (the pride of life). Eve placed her desire and lust above the command she received from the Lord, which caused her to sin. She allowed "self" to become the ruler of her life. Adam, in a likewise manner, did the same. Anytime someone places their fleshly desires (self-pleasure) in the driver's seat of their lives, it is sure to manufacture a destructive end. When "self" (fleshly and carnal appetites) are steering things, it will never result in a positive outcome. Instead, it will lead to disaster. Unfortunately, many people today allow these things to occur in their lives, allowing fleshly desires and appetites to dictate their conduct and behavior. These types of actions are often justified through human reasoning and rationale. However, when the lust of the flesh determines someone's course of action, it will always bring forth the fruit of sin regardless of carnal arguments.

The apostle Paul gave a strong directive to Christians. He said that we are to "crucify the flesh." That means it is to be

vi

put to death. King Self is to be nailed to a cross; it is to be asphyxiated and starved of its oxygen supply. We are to declare "death to selfie."

In *Death to Selfie*, Will Owen articulates clearly and concisely how you can overcome and conquer the works of the flesh. Through biblical precepts and real-life experiences, he marvelously takes the reader on a journey of triumph. This is not merely a book about how the flesh operates and functions but how you can overcome the flesh yourself. We know that Jesus overcame everything that satan hurled at Him. Likewise, you can embrace that same power and overcome it all. The truths in this book will equip and propel you to experience victory and triumph. You will be empowered to rise in faith as you declare that sin will not have dominion over your life. You will experience "death to selfie."

DEATH TO SELFIE

TABLE OF CONTENTS

DEATH TO SELFIE

INTRODUCTION

As I write this introduction, it's not even the same decade in which I began the journey of writing this book. In fact, it has been over twelve years since the first words were put to paper. In that time, a lot has changed—some for good and some for the not-so-good.

One of the more recent trends within our culture here in the U.S. is the inspiration for a portion of the title of this book: the "selfie"—a self-taken photograph shared with the world via social media. This relatively new method for sharing life events and special moments with friends and family has revealed something that resides within each of us to some degree or another. For some, it indicates vanity; for others, it may be materialism. It could be a number of things, but at its root, the common problem that each of us must confront and ultimately deal with is SELF.

SELF is the soil from which every root of sin first springs and the subject I'll address most as you read this book. As believers mature, we must begin to put our default sinful nature to death and live our lives selflessly as Jesus did. If we can truly accomplish this, we will fulfill God's greatest calling on our lives, which is to love God and love our neighbor as ourselves.

As we progress from chapter to chapter, you will be taken systematically through the process of analyzing the common problem we all must face: our tendency to focus more on ourselves and less on others. We then take a deep dive into the roots of the problem, which begins with our enemy, the devil. In the case study on satan, we'll learn how he acts and his motivations. In order to recognize his lies and influence, it is best to know our enemy and quickly identify him in any situation. Next, we'll study Jesus, the answer to the problem. We will learn how Jesus exhibited selfless behavior and set the pattern for us all to follow. With the aid of the Holy Spirit and our Bibles, we have been equipped to live our lives as Jesus did, selflessly and ultimately sinlessly. Finally, in the last chapters, you'll get a practical application of the solution. The roadmap comes together, and you'll have clear instructions on how you can begin living your life above sin. Ultimately it is the desire of this author to see us all fulfill our highest calling, which is to serve others as we do ourselves.

Are you ready to begin this journey with me? Let's start the process of bringing "death to selfie."

SECTION
1

A COMMON PROBLEM TO BE SOLVED

DEATH TO SELFIE

1

UNDERSTANDING THE SELF-NATURE

(OUR COMMON PROBLEM)

As believers, we often hear the word "flesh" being used in reference to the thing that causes us to miss the mark or sin. In Christian circles, "flesh" has been used extensively for hundreds of years since the Bible was translated into English. But, unfortunately, it has lost some of the true and accurate understanding it once conveyed. *Flesh* is best defined according to *Strong's Dictionary*: "The flesh denotes mere human nature, the earthly nature of man apart from divine influence, and therefore prone to sin and opposed to God."

As I began to pray over this idea of "flesh" and the way it is used, it became evident that I did not understand it as well as I thought. So, I studied and prayed more about the word and its use, and I realized that the flesh is the same thing as selfishness. I understood the word "selfishness" much better than the word *flesh*. However, I had failed to pay much attention to selfishness in my own life since I thought it was not as egregious as other sins.

For example, one form of notable egregious sinful behavior could be the act of physically assaulting another person. Anyone would agree that you should not hit or punch another human being; it's an awful thing to do. Stealing is also universally agreed upon without argument as a terrible sin and something we should not do. These things are always relegated in our minds as really bad things, and the truth is, they are!

Once the revelation of "flesh" being "self" was opened up to me, I began to realize that I had dramatically underestimated the significance of "selfish behavior." The truth is that selfishness can be found at the root of every sin ever committed since the beginning of time. Therefore, if we ranked immoral behaviors, selfishness should be at the top of the list because it is the root cause of all sinful behavior.

Upon further reflection, I began to realize that I was under the assumption that my "flesh" was something from which I could not separate myself due to it being an intrinsic part of my nature. There is a measure of truth in that manner of thinking. Apart from divine influence, one cannot separate themselves from their carnal desires due to the weight of that dominant force toward sinful behavior. A prevailing sensual influence that operates within the earth and our culture in this present age. Although our flesh cannot be done away with while we are here on this earth, it does not grant us a license to continue in sinful behavior.

As I studied, I began to think, *"What if this inclination to sin could be removed?"* I pondered if it was possible that the very influence to sin could be silenced or rendered powerless. It was during this time of reflection that I realized our flesh could be put to death. We'll talk more about this later.

Sin's Roots and Definition

There is a universal trait that all humans share, and that trait is self. It has been referred to in the past as flesh, but for this book *self* will be used in its place. The Lord clearly told me, "**Self is the root of all sin.**" I bolded and underlined this to save you the effort. I would recommend that you commit that statement to memory. The inward focus we have on ourselves, driven by selfish desires, is what causes us to sin.

Sin is defined as missing the mark. Here's a good analogy to help you understand sin. Imagine an archer shooting at a circular target one hundred paces away. His "mark" or aim is the middle of the center circle. His target is a small circle with little area to hit at any significant distance away from the target. Think of what a shot it would be to strike the right of the target when standing a hundred paces away from it! Even though it was a great shot, it still missed the mark. This example is the picture of sin. Sin is to miss the mark, no matter how small or large the margin of error. That is why God doesn't rank sins. Missing the mark is missing the mark.

What Does the Bible Say about the World We Live in Today?

We can all agree that our society and culture in the United States today are not walking in the Spirit as the Bible instructs. On the contrary, the way of the world has always been to walk in the flesh. For those who may not be familiar with Christian jargon, to "walk in the flesh" means that we carry out our lives in a manner directed or controlled by our carnal desires. To "walk in the flesh" is to allow oneself to be led in any direction our natural minds permit.

Conversely, to "walk in the Spirit" is to be Spirit-led or Holy Spirit-led. Said another way, this means that we adhere to instruction and counsel that comes from God, both through His written Word (Holy Spirit breathed and inspired) and also His five-fold ministry (God's hand in the earth), which are His apostles, prophets, pastors, teachers, and evangelists. But it does not stop there. It also includes allowing ourselves to be led by the voice of the Holy Spirit, which will always agree with the written Word and five-fold ministers to whom you've submitted for counsel.

I believe it is safe to say that we are living in the last days about which Paul writes in his letters to Timothy. In 2 Timothy, Paul admonishes Timothy to be mindful of the things to come and wise to the behavior of those the enemy has influenced. The New King James Version reads this way:

> But know this, that in the last days perilous times will come: For men will be lovers of themselves, lovers of money, boasters, proud, blasphemers, disobedient to parents, unthankful, unholy, unloving, unforgiving, slanderers, without self-control, brutal, despisers of good, traitors, headstrong, haughty, lovers of pleasure rather than lovers

of God, having a form of godliness but denying its power. And from such people turn away (2 Timothy 3:1-5).

I find it interesting that in each example of sinful behavior in this passage, self is at the root of it all. To love money is to love what money can bring to self. To be boastful is to broadcast one's own greatness or the importance connected to one's self. To be disobedient to a parent is to act as satan did when he disobeyed God. It's the created rising up to defy the Creator. In this, we see self-exaltation above genuine authority. I could expound upon each example, but I think the point is made. Self is at the root of all sinful behavior. We must be awakened to this fact and see selfishness in the proper light.

Biblical Examples of Selfishness in Manifestation

Biblical examples of selfishness in manifestation are found in many more of Paul's teachings. Paul is responsible for writing more than half of the New Testament, so it is fair to say he had a great deal of revelation on the subject of flesh and the works of the flesh. Paul writes:

> I say then: Walk in the Spirit, and you shall not fulfill the lust of the flesh. For the flesh lusts against the Spirit and the Spirit against the flesh; and these are contrary to one another, so that you do not do the things that you wish. But if you are led by the Spirit, you are not under the law. Now the works of the flesh are evident, which are: adultery,

fornication, uncleanness, lewdness, idolatry, sorcery, hatred, contentions, jealousies, outbursts of wrath, selfish ambitions, dissensions, heresies, envy, murders, drunkenness, revelries, and the like; of which I tell you beforehand, just as I told you in the time past, that those who practice such things will not inherit the kingdom of God (Galatians 5:16-21).

It is clearly understood by anyone who names the name of Jesus that these "works of the flesh" Paul is writing about are sins, and these things should not be practiced in the life of a believer. The revelation that came to me and helped me to better apply this teaching in my own life is that the "works of the flesh" are the same as saying the "works of selfishness." When read and understood this way, one can take personal ownership of their behavior. I always thought the flesh was unchangeable, and therefore, I was powerless to escape the behavior. The enemy wants us to believe that sinful behavior is simply our lot in life and that we cannot stand up to it. By taking ownership of sinful behavior and calling it what it is, selfishness, we can begin to strip it from our lives and see sin's power reduced and even completely eradicated.

Modern Examples of the Self-Nature at Work

With this understanding of the self-nature (flesh-nature) being the thing that drives you toward sinful behavior, let's look at some examples that we can observe in today's culture here in America.

1. Ministers of the gospel are routinely making a mockery of themselves by getting caught in scandalous affairs made public for the world to see. The self-nature has gripped many church leaders by luring them with carnal things that promise to bring something desirable to self.

2. The self-nature has convinced some gospel ministers that it is better to seat more people on Sunday than to face potential rejection by preaching the uncompromised Word of God. The spirit of compromise has infiltrated the church through the exaltation of self, and the Word of God has been watered down to fit the modern culture.

3. The self-nature has caused men and women of God to be concerned only with themselves without being a light in a dark world. Many Christians in America have become self-centered with no care for the lost and dying.

4. A new generation of young people is turning their backs on the Church because, in their minds, it wreaks of bigotry and hypocrisy. Unfortunately, many parents and church leaders have failed to example godly leadership to these up-and-coming believers. This manifestation of the self-nature in parents and leaders has robbed the youth of their desire to connect to the church.

5. Churches throughout the U.S. are dying out because new young families are not being added to aging congregations. The self-nature has told an older generation that everyone must conform to their way of doing things because it is better. This belief causes them to fail at making room for a new generation, allowing them to springboard from the previous generation's wisdom.

6. The self-nature has caused pastors to replace God-given vision with selfish ambition to the point that they lose their families in the process. Self, in the form of "my ministry," gets promoted over the family and ultimately leads to destruction. Unfortunately, pastors' children become victims and the butt of jokes almost universally.

7. The Church is more divided than ever before. The self-nature has produced strife and division in local churches everywhere, resulting in church splits and the Absalom spirit in manifestation. Agreement and unity are qualities that have seemingly disappeared within the body of Christ at large.

8. Loving others, which is required to truly love God, seems absent many American believers today. Instead, the self-nature has caused many to focus on their own lives to such a degree that many are blinded to those who are hurting and need help.

9. Spiritual lethargy has gripped many in the church today, causing many to sit on the sidelines while watching others do the work of the ministry. The self-nature has deceived many into relinquishing their own responsibility in the Kingdom and irresponsibly transferring it to those in full-time ministry.

10. Dads are losing families to their ambitions. The self-nature has turned the heads of many fathers, making it difficult to see clearly life's most important priorities. As a result, many dads fail to fulfill their home responsibility, forcing moms to do things they were not intended to do and filling shoes they were not created to fill.

11. The self-nature has lied to men causing them to believe they have a right to leave (divorce) their families. At the same time, the self-nature has lied to women telling them they can do it all on their own, adding fuel to the fire.

12. Pornography is at epidemic levels in the lives of many people within our society. The self-nature has said to both men and women that other people's lives are unimportant. They desire a moment of pleasure regardless of the consequence to the person entertaining them. They are either ignorant or callous to the destruction that their selfish choice has created. The human being upon which they cast their lustful gaze often lives a life of destitution, loss, tragedy, fear, shame, and hopelessness, enslaved to the industry, figuratively or literally. The self-nature glorifies self-gratification at the expense of the person from whom they are objectifying.

13. Many are propagating a message of God's grace as something that allows you to sin. The self-nature says that living a blameless, spotless, holy life is far too difficult and requires too much effort.

14. Some church leaders tolerate homosexuality and even encourage it in some cases. Unfortunately, the self-nature has crept in and caused men and women of God to listen to the lie of political correctness and allow that spirit to cloud their judgment. All this is based on the idea that standing for what the Bible says will ultimately lead to fewer people in the congregation or even their own dismissal.

These things and so many more are real-world evidence that the self-nature is very much alive in every area where we see things in disorder.

The Land Flowing with Milk and Honey

The culture or society that we live in as Americans is completely self-absorbed. We have every luxury and more abundance than we could ever need—the land that flows with milk and honey. Our nation is so blessed that even our poorest citizens are comparable to the middle class in third-world countries. We have no loss or lack for any individual wanting to work. There is no limit to where any person can go and no boundary on what they can earn.

Most of us have multiple cars. We have homes with running water and electricity. Electric appliances do most of the mundane chores for us. Closets are full of clothing that we do not wear, toys that are not played with, and shoes that are hardly used. Food rots in the refrigerator, movie stockpiles are sitting on shelves, and garages are so full that we can't park our cars in them.

Where amid this opulent wealth (and that is what it is to the rest of the world) is the thought for anyone else but ourselves? I asked this question, and I was ashamed of myself. Here I am, thinking that I am this guy with his head screwed on straight. I live a holy life, or so I thought. I am in church every time the doors are open, functioning in many different areas of ministry. I visit the prisons, serve on my church board, and am faithful in tithing and giving offerings. I could continue talking about the areas where I felt like I was doing what was right. Truthfully, those were all good things and should be done. However, what had I done to ensure I looked outward by thinking of others?

The biblical truth is that you can give without loving, but you can't love without giving. John 3:16 says, "God so loved the world that He gave..." and 1 John 4:20 says you can't love God without loving your brother. The apostle Paul said that if he could sing with the voice of angels, it would be like sounding brass or a clanging cymbal if love was absent.

If we must give to love, our American culture has much to learn. Most Americans are self-seeking to their core. When a culture is blessed with the wealth that America possesses, it becomes easy to fall into the trap of selfishness and self-seeking when we begin to place our focus on the comforts that come with our blessings. The fear of losing those comforts drives us to take measures to prevent their loss instead of putting our focus on Him, who gives us the blessings in the first place.

In America, it seems like every commercial you see on TV and hear on the radio is focused on getting you more of this, a faster that, a more beautiful you, a happier you, a slimmer you, etc. These messages place the focus on YOU.

Our modern culture's self-seeking way of life is nothing more than a product of many generations living in a selfish fleshly pursuit of "perceived" happiness. Notice that the word perceived is emphasized. Happiness is a good thing; everyone wants to be happy. We should be encouraged to know that the happiness we seek is possible and not far from us but may manifest in a way that differs from what we expected.

The examples mentioned earlier in this chapter and countless others reveal how the self-nature manifests itself in everyday life. In the following pages, we will identify the self-nature at work. Then, with the help of the Holy Spirit, we can all turn and go in a different direction.

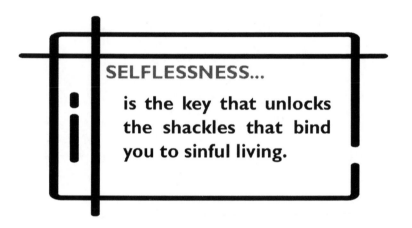

SELFLESSNESS...

is the key that unlocks the shackles that bind you to sinful living.

2
KNOW YOUR ENEMY

Have you ever heard the phrase "operating under the influence"? This phrase is used to describe someone who has been drinking alcohol and driving a car. Drunk drivers, as they are called, operate their vehicles dangerously, often swerving in and out of their lanes. Many times, they drive at an excessive rate of speed, endangering their own lives and the lives of others. Yet, these same drivers likely drive skillfully and within legal speed limits when sober. Under an outside influence, they often fail to obey traffic laws or are impaired to such a degree that they are not physically able to operate their vehicle safely. The drivers are much like any other driver, except that their mind is affected by an outside influence. Their bloodstream is saturated with alcohol which has the effect of thinning the blood that subjects the brain to a myriad of feelings and emotions, leaving their judgment impaired. Eventually, as the alcohol works through the body, it is absorbed, and the brain begins to function as it did before the introduction of the outside influence.

Just like the analogy of the driver operating under the influence of alcohol, your mind is subject to a very real spiritual influence present today in this age. Our self-nature exists because of satan's influence on the earth beginning when he and one-third of the angels were exiled here by God and granted limited authority, according to the Bible. Satan is referred to as the god of this age (2 Corinthians 4:4) and the ruler of this age (John 12:31, NLT).

While satan operates here in his realm, our minds and spirits are exposed to his influence from the moment we arrive until the moment we leave this earth. There is no escaping this influence. We cannot simply pray the devil away and expect him to remain silent for the rest of our days. Christians have the ability to silence the enemy, and there is much teaching in the Word about this subject. However, we cannot mute him or his minions indefinitely. He is on the earth during this age, and there is a reason for his existence and presence here.

We must understand that God created satan. God sent him here when he fell; He could have destroyed him, but He did not do that. Instead, God exiled satan to Earth, and while here, he possesses limited authority and has the ability to influence each of us. However, there is good news! There is a greater influence available to us. We'll discuss this more in a later chapter.

Genesis includes the definitive plan and purpose for humanity. Mankind was created in God's likeness and image to rule the earth, subdue it, and steward over it (Genesis 1:26-28). God desired to create man for fellowship with Him. The Lord told Adam and Eve that they could have anything they wanted in the Garden of Eden and only forbade them from the Tree of the

Knowledge of Good and Evil. Before eating from the fruit of this tree, there was no realization of sin or evil; they could not discern it. There was no temptation because man had not yet been separated from God. Man was in close fellowship with God, so he imitated his closest influence. The presence of God will cause you to be drawn toward God's way. It will cause you to act like God, imitate God, and be a doer of what God said to do.

Sin's Origin

> For we do not wrestle against flesh and blood, but against principalities, against powers, against the rulers of the darkness of this age, against spiritual hosts of wickedness in the heavenly places (Ephesians 6:12).

Sin began when the enemy was cast to the earth. According to Revelation 20, when satan is locked away for a thousand years, there will be no sin because the influence to sin will have been removed. Sin will cease once the urge to sin is no longer present. There is a real revelation in this! Jesus came to earth to break sin's power and restore man's relationship with God as it was in the beginning.

When Adam & Eve sinned, it placed a wall between God and man. It caused the closeness they shared to become separated. An alternate influence was introduced when humanity was exposed to the knowledge of good and evil. For millennia, this alternate influence was the dominant influence on Earth. Satan, along with his demonic horde, was on the earth long before man and woman.

So, what does the self-nature resemble today? It looks like it has always looked since sin first entered the world. The self-nature is the self-serving tendency of man's heart, absent of God's influence. The self-nature is the inward-looking tendency of man's heart tuned to satan's influence—the ruler of this world. With this understanding, we can begin to see the true source of our weakness with open eyes. It lies within our own *choice* to allow the enemy's influence, which manifests itself as our self-nature (flesh), to be most prevalent in our lives.

Influence

Every human being functions as a product of their influences. Each man, woman, boy, and girl all function as the sum of our collective influences. In math, the term "sum" is used to denote the combining of two individual numbers: two plus two equals the sum of four. The way you function in your life is the sum of influences throughout your life up until now.

The very language you speak is a direct result of your influences. For example, when you were born into this world, the people surrounding you probably spoke one language. If you were born in America, English words were likely spoken to you each day. As a result of constantly hearing these words, your dialect became like those you heard. If you were born into a Japanese family living in Japan, the odds are that you would speak Japanese, and if you were born into a Russian family living in Russia, you would likely speak Russian.

I used this example to emphasize that we all respond to our collective influences. I also want to place the spotlight on one specific **universal influence** that each of us must address. This influence is not physical; we cannot see, touch, taste, smell, or hear it with our natural ears. It is **satan's influence** on the earth that is the culprit behind our self-nature, and it is his **influence** that causes sin to persist even though Jesus has already broken sin's power.

If you don't believe that "every" human being is exposed to this influence, just sit and watch a group of four small children playing together with three toys. How much fighting do you think there will be over a worthless piece of plastic while each child attempts to take it from the others to bring themselves joy? From the time we come out of the womb until the day we are laid to rest, we are exposed to the influence of the prince of the power of the air, satan. His influence causes sinful behavior to manifest in our lives.

Satan: A Case Study

Let's do a study on satan for a moment to ensure we have a complete understanding of our enemy and what his method of operation or modus operandi (MO) entails.
The prophet Isaiah, speaking with the voice of God through the inspiration of the Holy Spirit, tells of Lucifer's motive to overthrow the kingdom of God:

> "For you have said in your heart: 'I will ascend into heaven, I will exalt my throne above the stars of God; I will also sit on the mount of the congregation On the farthest sides of the north; I will ascend above the heights of the clouds, I will be like the Most High'" (Isaiah 14:13-14).

Lucifer's signature, or his MO, is to seek an elevated position **above** God. The prophet Isaiah even tells us that he sought to be just like God, a temptation that the serpent threw at Eve in the Garden of Eden.

Another instance of satan's signature being exposed is found in Ezekiel, "**Your** heart was lifted up because of **your** beauty; **You** corrupted **your** wisdom for the sake of **your** splendor;" (Ezekiel 28:17). This passage of Scripture is directly pointed to satan as symbolized by the king of Tyre. In this passage, satan is so consumed with "self" that it corrupts his wisdom.

In Job chapter 1, we see satan reasoning with God as to why Job serves the Lord. What does the enemy say? He says that Job only fears the Lord because the He has blessed him. What kind of mind must you possess to make a statement like that? Satan believed that Job was faithful because he was blessed; he accused Job of caring only for himself. In this accusation, satan exposes his true motives or his true core principles; he is "SELF" DRIVEN.

You can search the entire Word of God and look for every instance of sin, and you will always trace it back to one thing: SELF. Self is the root of all sin. SELF spelled backward is **FLES,** one letter shy of FLESH. Interesting.

Let's move forward to Matthew chapter four, where Jesus had been fasting for 40 days, and satan came to tempt Him. What is the first temptation? He used bread, which Christ's body was agonizing for at that moment. Satan was attempting to get Jesus to shift His focus from outward-looking to something that would appeal to His flesh.

Satan's second attack was to question Jesus' identity. He said, *"If you are who you say you are..."* This is to point the finger in God's face and doubt the Almighty! Who could challenge the Son of the Most High God? To question God is to put your "self" in a place of equality with Him. The enemy again shows us his innermost thoughts with his words; satan thinks he's equal to God. How many of us have questioned God? We must guard against this, for if we do not, we are in jeopardy of receiving the same sentence satan received.

Satan says to Jesus in a final attack, *"Submit—bow down—to me, and I will give you all the kingdoms of this world."* We observe that satan wants to be **above** God. He wants to put God beneath himself—he wants to rise above Him.

In every temptation, Jesus overcame. He triumphed over the enemy because He would not yield to flesh or self. As we read these accounts, it allows us to observe and learn how satan seeks to exert his influence within the lives of people today. Jesus recognized satan's strategies and would not yield to them.

> We wrestle not against flesh and blood, but against principalities and powers and the **rulers** of the darkness of this age, against spiritual wickedness in the heavenly places (Ephesians 6:12, emphasis added).

When satan was sent to the earth with his demonic horde, he was given limited authority, and while he is still here, he roams about like a roaring lion, seeking whom he may devour (1 Peter 5:8). We must understand that satan's job is to rule this earth by way of his influence.

> But even if our gospel is veiled, it is veiled to
> those who are perishing, whose minds **the god
> of this age** has blinded, who do not believe, lest
> the light of the gospel of the glory of Christ,
> who is the image of God, should shine on them
> (2 Corinthians 4:3-4, emphasis added).

Satan's influence is evident when we observe the sinful behavior of anyone born on the earth from creation until now. Why do you think sin showed up? First, it was because satan sinned, and secondly, humanity was exposed to the knowledge of good and evil.

Let's look at the first instance of sin in the Bible. In the Garden of Eden, what did the serpent tell Eve? He said, *"If you eat this fruit, you will be like God."* This statement lured her into thinking about her-SELF, the exact same thing satan did just before he was evicted from heaven. He is encouraging her to look toward herself (Genesis 3:4).

What did satan do when he was tempting Jesus on the mountain? He was inviting Jesus to look toward Himself with the lure of the world's kingdoms in exchange for submission (Matthew 4:8).

In every instance of temptation or satanic influence in the entire Bible, you will see the enemy doing one thing. He either focuses on himself or influences others to look toward themselves. This behavior is the epitome of selfishness versus selflessness.

Proper Perspective on "Self"

In all this negative discussion on self, there could be a misunderstanding that self is bad. That is not the truth. Your "self" nature keeps you alive while you're on this earth. You are always protecting your "self" from danger, like seeing that you eat so you don't starve. You see that your interests, such as money, possessions, family relationships, etc., are preserved. You ensure you have a job and transportation—that your family has what they need to be safe and secure. Each of these things is tied to self, which is good when kept in proper order

We always have to realize that the enemy is a perverter. Eve's hunger was legitimate. However, eating the wrong fruit was an unlawful means to fulfill her appetite. The enemy will appeal to the flesh through an illegitimate means to meet a legitimate need.

The Over-Under Hand Drill

> "Yet it shall not be so among you; but whoever desires **to become great among you, let him be your servant**. And whoever desires to be first among you, let him be your slave—just as the Son of Man did not come to be served, but to serve, and to give His life a ransom for many" (Matthew 20:26-28, emphasis added).

We must keep this one truth in the forefront of our minds if we are to truly find happiness in this life, and that is to place our focus directly on the words of Christ when He said to be great is to be the servant of all. In this one sentence lies the true hidden secret of the gospel. It is one

23

simple flip of our thinking—from attempting to be over someone to placing one's self under.

Let's do an exercise that will help visualize how the enemy's influence works. First, place your right hand horizontally in front of you. Your right hand represents God the Father. Now take your left hand, which represents you, and put it above your right hand. This is a picture of what the devil attempted to do prior to being kicked out of heaven. Now place your left hand beneath your right hand. This is a picture of what Jesus exemplified when He came to earth, living fully submitted to His Father.

On the earth, God has appointed leaders within the Church to lead, guide, and be the conduit by which He educates believers on how they should live and function in their spiritual lives. 1 Peter 5:6 says, "Therefore humble yourselves under the mighty hand of God, that He may exalt you in due time." In some cases, these leaders will mentor and train people on how to live their natural lives. The leaders within the Church are apostles, prophets, pastors, evangelists, and teachers. In Ephesians, we read:

> And He himself gave some to be apostles, some
> prophets, some evangelists; and some pastors
> and teachers, For the equipping of the saints for
> the work of the ministry, for the edifying of the
> body of Christ; (Ephesians 4:11-13).

My pastor refers to the five-fold ministry offices as the hand of God in the earth, with each office symbolizing a finger of the hand. While performing this exercise about how you submit to God, put those leaders who are in positions of authority in your life within the right hand and then place your left hand underneath illustrating, *"I will submit to the teaching of my pastor"* and with the perspective, *"I will faithfully execute my pastor's advice and counsel"* (as long as it is godly counsel based on Scripture). This exercise works equally well when you place any of the other four ministry offices in place of the pastor. The correct response should be to submit to their teaching because they watch out for your soul.

> Have confidence in your leaders and submit to their authority, because they keep watch over you as those who must give an account. Do this so that their work will be a joy, not a burden, for that would be of no benefit to you (Hebrews 13:17, NIV).

If we can successfully place ourselves underneath the mighty hand of God both spiritually and naturally, we align ourselves in proper order to be guided and directed toward blessing, honor, favor, and happiness.

The Deception of the Enemy

Let's look at a few common scenarios where the deception of the enemy is at work.

Scenario 1: A man chooses to work 70 hours a week under the guise of *"I'm doing this to benefit my family."* In turn, he loses the relationship he had with his family before he began working long hours. What do you suppose his true motive was if he were to continue working that way? I would say that it was selfish gain or a desire for something that the money might bring to "self." We must understand that the enemy will not lure us with bait that looks like a trap or snare. Instead, he is going to entice us with things like, *"This is for little Johnny"* or *"If I do this, I will be helping my family."*

When Jesus was born, we see the enemy's attack through Herod's deception (Matthew 2:7-8). This is another example of "self" winning out. Herod does not want to be replaced and fears the loss of his rule; he tells the wise men that he wants to go and worship the babe. That sounds like a good thing, right? What could be wrong with going to worship the Son of God? Herod hopes the wise men will divulge the location of this newborn babe, so he can kill it before having the chance to grow up. The enemy continues to use this type of deception, even in little things like everyday decision-making. We must be on guard and ready to say "NO" when temptation presents itself. Allowing selfishness to rule your life will ultimately lead to destruction, just like it did for Herod.

Does this tactic mean that we can't make our own decisions? No, it does not. You don't need to neglect and bring harm or loss to yourself while learning to obey God's Word. However, consulting trusted advisors could benefit you as you make choices that possibly impact others. If we look at the big picture—the future impact—of our decision-making, we can align ourselves with Jesus' instructions to be servants of all.

Scenario 2: If a man wants to take his family on vacation, he has the right to do so. But, if his decision to go on vacation conflicts with the family's current financial situation, he has allowed the "self" nature to prevail over good judgment. Selfish thinking would sacrifice the family's needs on the altar of "bless your family **now**." Righteous thinking rightly divides the word of truth by saying, *"I want to be a blessing to my family, and we will save up for this vacation so that it will be the true blessing it is meant to be."*

Scenario 3: Dad has been daydreaming about buying a boat—dreaming of waking up early, unrestrained, with no distractions for a day of quiet and peace. He dreams of spending time on the lake, all alone with his rod, reel, and the Holy Ghost, trolling the lake and landing the big one that will make all the guys jealous. Can you imagine this fellow? He's rubbing his hands together with a sly grin as he backs the truck up to the boat to hitch it up. For the record, fishing is a good thing—nothing wrong with it—some of Jesus' best men were fishermen. But what if the family took a back seat to the financial obligation of this new boat? Would the family lose too much daddy time? Could the family resent the boat because their father was more excited about it than he was about them? When is the most opportune time to go out on the boat? For most of us, that would be Saturday morning. When are the kids at home? When does your wife need you most? Can you see the picture?

"Self" will drive you to look to your own needs, wants, and desires instead of your true responsibilities, where your attention should be firmly planted. The balance of this scenario could be varied. For example, dad could buy a boat when the budget allows without sacrificing the kids' college funds or when there is sufficient income to not feel the loss from such an expensive purchase. Or, dad could buy a boat that could be enjoyed by the entire family, which possesses amenities that everyone can enjoy--not a fishing boat with two seats.

Can you see the point that I am making here? You can have what you desire, but it must be in line with what is righteous and what is in order. Therefore, your decisions must be ordered to the Word of God and not based on selfish impulses.

I once heard a minister say that he had counseled many young people throughout his ministry. In nearly every counseling session, the complaints he heard were not, *"Daddy didn't buy me an iPad®"* or *"Daddy didn't buy me a BMW®."* Instead, it was, *"Daddy left mama!"* The picture painted was one of selfish desire on the part of the father instead of thinking about what was righteous and best for all parties involved.

I know many have been through this situation, and these words are not meant to condemn anyone. But, from this day forward, we should operate with this attitude: *"I will act selflessly and not selfishly. I will think of others and not myself only."*

In the situation where dad left mom, it could have been for selfish reasons, or it could have been for legitimate reasons. Either way, the result is the same. The children suffer because of the decision to split.

So, what is the answer in this situation? Jesus said that to be great in the kingdom of heaven, you would become least among all your brethren and that you would become a servant of all. That means these parents should seek reconciliation instead of divorce. Through this selfless act, they lay the foundation upon which they build a stable home where the children have a well-balanced upbringing. In a structured and well-rounded environment, the children can understand who they are in Christ and in their own families. The products of a selfless choice to reconcile are the children who grow up without all the destructive emotional baggage and rebellious attitude that always comes with something so life-altering as divorce.

How Do We Serve

Serving others does not necessarily mean getting a job waiting tables in a restaurant. Instead, it means considering another's needs and seeking to be a blessing to them when possible. We will go into more detail about servanthood in a later chapter.

There is hope for those who see this situation as hopeless. Don't let the enemy tell you otherwise; don't let him tell you that it will be too hard. It will be challenging, but God will not require anything of you that you can't bear; He is there to help. If you are persistent and do not give up, you will reap a harvest. That is God's promise.

"And let us not grow weary while doing good, for in due season we shall reap if we do not lose heart" (Galatians 6:9).

Throughout Scripture, God's words are repeated in one way, shape, or form. God spoke to me recently and said, "All the Word is a symphony." He then began to show me that each book of the Bible is like one instrument within a symphony orchestra. Each musical instrument is different, yet they all play the same song. From instrument to instrument, the notes may not be played in the same order or tone, yet each is in harmony with the entirety of the orchestra. It is beautiful beyond measure when all the instruments come together in the same song, in a common key, and played with skill and discipline. As we learn more about the "self" nature, we begin to think of the entire Word of God, all pointing to one thing: to be great is to be least. To be high is to put your "self" beneath. To be honored is to let someone else celebrate you, not to honor your "self."

"For all the law is fulfilled in one word, even in this: 'You shall love your neighbor as yourself'" (Galatians 5:14).

Jesus is the most honored name of all time. He is also the only human that ever sought to place Himself completely beneath all others, even willingly submitting Himself to death on the cross. Everything Jesus did exemplified how we should submit to God; He demonstrated love and fulfilled the commandments of God.

To overcome self, we must learn to love others more than ourselves. To live as Jesus lived, we must say NO to our flesh and YES to His will.

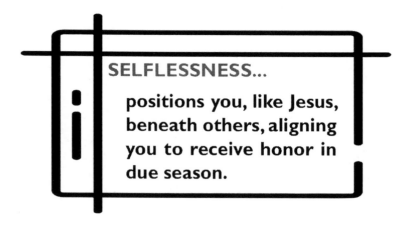

SELFLESSNESS...

positions you, like Jesus, beneath others, aligning you to receive honor in due season.

SECTION 2

HOW THE PROBLEM IS MANIFESTED

DEATH TO SELFIE

3

THE LUST OF THE FLESH

Satan's tactics in this world, or "during this age," as the Bible refers to it, have not changed since day one. Satan is incapable of creating anything new; all he can do is pervert the truth or manipulate what is already in existence. Satan uses three methods to influence souls that dwell on the earth. In this chapter, we will focus on the lust of the flesh, but before we do, let's look at what the Bible says about these three methods.

The Bible is clear on what the world has to offer, and three different Bible references spell out satan's methods. Therefore, it is essential to understand that each time you experience an attack from the enemy, it will manifest in one of these three ways, all of which point back to SELF.

The **first** account is found in Genesis 3, at the beginning of all life as we know it, when the serpent is tempting Eve with the Tree of the Knowledge of good and evil. Let's read it:

> When the woman saw that the fruit of the tree
> was **good for food** and **pleasing to the eye**, and
> also **desirable for gaining wisdom**, she took

some and ate it. She also gave some to her
husband, who was with her, and he ate it
(Genesis 3:6, NIV, emphasis added).

The **second** account is found in Matthew 4 when satan is
tempting Jesus on the mountain that we mentioned in
chapter two. Satan, referred to as the tempter, attempts to
entice Jesus with bread—the lust of the flesh, with things—
the lust of the eye, and finally, with compromise in
exchange for personal exaltation.

The **third** account is illustrated when John says, "For all
that is in the world—the lust of the flesh, the lust of the
eyes, and the pride of life—is not of the Father but is of the
world" (1 John 2:16).

Where It All Began

Let's look closer at the first account of these three
temptations found at the time of creation. In this passage of
Scripture, the serpent tempts Eve with these three things
spoken of by the apostle John.

> Now the serpent was more cunning than any
> beast of the field which the Lord God had
> made. And he said to the woman, "Has God
> indeed said, 'You shall not eat of every tree of
> the garden'?" And the woman said to the
> serpent, "We may eat the fruit of the trees of
> the garden; but of the fruit of the tree which is
> in the midst of the garden, God has said, 'You
> shall not eat it, nor shall you touch it, lest you
> die.'" Then the serpent said to the woman, "You

will not surely die. For God knows that in the
day you eat of it your eyes will be opened, and
you will be like God, knowing good and evil."
So when the woman saw that the tree was good
for food, that it was pleasant to the eyes, and a
tree desirable to make one wise, she took of its
fruit and ate. She also gave some to her husband
with her, and he ate (Genesis 3:1-6).

The fruit was pleasing to the eye, which is indicative of the
lust of the eye. It was good for food, which illustrates the
lust of the flesh. Finally, the tree was desirable to make one
wise, depicting the pride of life. This powerful connection
can be seen from the beginning of Scripture to the end of
the Bible; the attack has not changed. The enemy of our
soul has not changed; it is the same old routine. He tries to
influence us, and we are capable of being influenced. The
question is, to which influence will we submit?

What Is the Lust of the Flesh

The "lust of the flesh" draws you to it by appealing to your
desires, such as food, sex, drugs, alcohol, and other tangible
things you can taste, smell, and feel. This drawing away
goes back to one common denominator, your "self." So
what is the reason the enemy uses these tactics? It is because
these are the same things that motivate satan himself. He is
present here on earth, so his way becomes the way of those
under his influence.

Satan imparts the lust of the flesh by way of his influence
so we may be moved away from our intended purpose here
on earth. In the case of the temptation to eat the forbidden

fruit, satan knew what was at stake if Adam and Eve made the mistake of partaking of it. God gave Adam and Eve explicit instructions to avoid consuming the fruit from this tree. Satan tempted them because he understood the consequences if they chose to eat the fruit.

God created Adam and Eve with a purpose that involved close communion with Him on a daily basis. This relationship could not exist in the presence of sin. God knew this and warned His creation of the dangers of eating from the Tree of the Knowledge of Good and Evil. The heavenly Father wanted what was best for His children; He was not trying to steal from them or prevent them from enjoying themselves. He was not lording His power over them or depriving them of any good thing. God wants what any good father wants for their children. He loves them and knows what is best for them while guiding them toward happiness, joy, peace, and prosperity.

As a father of three small children, I can tell you that my every action toward my children is rooted in leading them in the right way so they will one day grow up and live their lives successfully. My love for them drives me in this direction; it guides my words and actions. In the same way, our heavenly Father delivers His instructions for our making and not for our breaking.

Satan has one goal while here on the earth; he desires to cause as many souls as possible to join him and his fallen angels in waging war against his enemy, Jehovah God. His strategy is simple. Satan wants to distract you from your true God-given purpose and cause you to be ineffective in accomplishing it while you live on the earth. Satan exists; he is on the earth, and his presence here carries with it his influence and that of his fellow fallen angels. The Bible says that when satan was thrown out of heaven, a third of the angelic host was cast out with him (Revelation 12:4 and Revelation 12:9). If satan can exert his influence over you, be assured that he influences them as well. They will operate in the same manner as their lord, satan.

A Good Thing Used Out of Order

We must also be wise to the fact that though there may be good things here on Earth, we are only permitted to take part in them if they align with God's Word, or *The Instructions*, as I like to call them. The Bible is an instruction manual for life. The Creator of your soul, body, and spirit wrote it so you might know how to act. Do you think your creator might have some insight into how you function and what makes you tick? Since He does, I can guarantee that *The Instruction*s will guide you on the right course so that you function as intended, without error.

A common example of a good thing being used outside of order is sex. When enjoyed within the stability of a biblical covenant relationship of marriage between a man and a woman, it is a good thing. From day one, sex was ordained by God. However, when a man and woman come together outside the marriage covenant, a good thing can then cause destruction. For example, in addition to the spiritual consequences, sex outside of marriage can produce a child who does not have the proper foundation from which to grow and be taught and trained. In addition, a promiscuous man or woman who shares their bed with many can contract a sexually transmitted disease and spread it to others.

Another typical example is a young woman seeking a man's affection. She agrees to have sex with him before marriage, and her heart is broken when he leaves. A soul tie is formed from the union, and she can suffer from emotional problems such as trust and rejection issues for the rest of her life. All of this happened because a good thing was used out of order.

These illustrations are simple and commonplace. The bottom line is that the lust of the flesh is real, and we must begin to see that the "self" nature will cause us to fall victim to these temptations while under the rule of the flesh. Until we die to our flesh, repent, and allow the Holy Spirit to change us from the inside, we should not be surprised if we keep falling victim to the same old things.

Repentance

True repentance involves turning and going in a different direction. Repentance will produce good fruit that is confirmed in the life of a believer, which will validate the change of course within one's life. When someone gets genuinely saved, there will be fruit that comes forth which is evidence of their salvation. No one is perfect, and getting saved does not enable you to become the fullness of Christ all in one day. But, there is a heart change, and the old way in which you once operated is no longer the predominant force in your life. There is something new that motivates you, and that is the call to live your life at a higher level.

The lust of the flesh will cause you to want to fall back into old ways. The flesh-nature whispers, *"I'm single and lonely; I really need some affection."* The whisper of the enemy in the attack disguised as a private thought tells you, *"It's your right, and you need it. It's not bad—it's not off-limits; you deserve it."* Satan will not tempt you by using other ways because this is how he thinks. Therefore, he has no choice but to influence you in the same way he operates.

When we detect that a behavior is consistent with how the enemy operates, it empowers us to rise up and say, *"NO! I will not be like satan. I will not be duped by the same lie to which he fell prey."* By the power of God's grace, we can choose to rise above the influence of the enemy!

Grace Defined

If you've been saved for any length of time, you've likely heard the phrase "saved by grace." You might also have read or heard it taught that you're under grace and not under the law. Do you know the proper definition of the word "grace"? The word "grace" comes from the Greek word *charis*, which is defined in ***Thayer's Greek-English Lexicon:***

> Of the merciful kindness by which God, exerting his holy influence upon souls, turns them to Christ, keeps, strengthens, increases them in Christian faith, knowledge, affection, and kindles them to the exercise of the Christian virtues.

Strong's Bible Dictionary definition of *charis* is "the divine influence upon the heart, and its reflection in the life."

The Holy Spirit was sent here so we might have another INFLUENCE on our hearts and minds. The Holy Spirit is literally the influence of Father God upon our spirit man while we are here on the earth. What is even more encouraging is the fact that the Holy Spirit's influence is greater than the influence of the enemy. The Holy Spirit is the very heartbeat of God placed within our spirit and body! The Holy Spirit's influence is grace!

Grace Defeats the Lust of the Flesh

The enemy would have you think that there is no hope for you. Satan would have you feel hopeless that you could ever live your life as the Bible instructs and commands. But I am here to tell you that because the enemy is telling you something, you can take it to the bank that it is a lie! The Bible says that the devil is the father of all lies. So, you can be sure that if he is whispering in your ear, it is, at minimum, a distortion of truth and most likely the opposite.

The enemy does not want you to know that the very power of God, His Holy Spirit, is available to you today. God's grace is made manifest in our lives when we allow the Holy Spirit to have greater influence.

How do we do this, you may ask? There are three parts to allowing the Holy Spirit to become the greatest influence in our lives:

- Choose to listen to the instructions of God contained in the Bible. We must become students of the Word. We must consume it as we consume food daily!

- Heed the voice of the Holy Spirit, which you can discern if you have a relationship with Him and have been baptized in the Holy Spirit.

- Heed the counsel of legitimate spiritual leadership to whom you have submitted yourself, such as your pastor, apostle, preacher, teacher, or evangelist.

If the Holy Spirit is speaking to you, these three parts will always agree with one another, and the three will always lead you in the right paths. This is being led by the Spirit, and adherence to this instruction will bring blessing into your life and allow you to rise above the lust of the flesh.

All three of these voices must agree to be assured that the Holy Spirit is leading you. The Bible says in 1 John 4:1 that we should test the spirits. To say it another way, we should not simply presume that any time we think we have heard from the Holy Spirit, we are correct in our perception. Since the Holy Spirit, on most occasions, does not speak to us audibly, we can misinterpret what we have heard with our spiritual ears. Therefore, it is essential for these voices to agree with one another: the Word, Spirit, and spiritual leadership. This agreement will ensure that we are being led by the Holy Spirit.

Understanding these truths is of tremendous significance, and applying this wisdom in our lives is paramount to our walk with the Lord. I first learned this balanced approach to discerning the voice of the Lord from my pastor. He mastered it over numerous years of study and teaching by leaders in the church. If we can place value on what the previous generations have learned and shared with us and then activate it within our lives, we will accelerate our learning curve and position ourselves for greater usefulness within the kingdom of God.

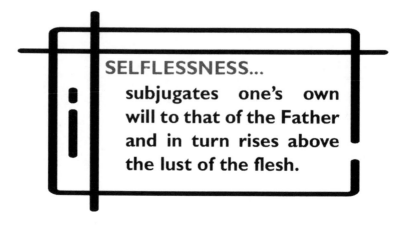

SELFLESSNESS...
subjugates one's own will to that of the Father and in turn rises above the lust of the flesh.

4

THE LUST OF THE EYE

"For all that is in the world—the lust of the flesh,
the lust of the eyes, and the pride of life—is not of the
Father but is of the world" (1 John 2:16).

When John wrote the above Scripture, he was echoing the
same three things that Eve fell for when she took the fruit
from the Tree of the Knowledge of good and evil. Eve saw
that the fruit was good for food, pleasing to the eye, and
the tree could make one wise. The second portion of this
trio is the focus of this chapter: the lust of the eye. I also
like to refer to this as the "lust of things for I." Since every
sin is rooted in selfishness, we will use this chapter to focus
on the enemy's way of thinking, specifically satan's
deception, that acquiring things will bring happiness and
joy. Ultimately, people who are ruled by their flesh will buy
into this deception because the prevailing influence in their
lives will dictate their actions.

What Is the Lust of the Eye?

The word "lust" in Greek is defined this way: "desire,
craving, longing, and a desire for what is forbidden." The
phrase "of the eye" is defined as "metaphorically the eyes of

the mind, the faculty of knowing." We can put these thoughts together and transliterate the phrase this way, "The longing or craving for natural things which appeal to our minds." This could be anything ranging from a sporty car to a large yacht, a new home, designer clothing, etc. All these things listed are good, and none of them could be considered taboo or off-limits if you are simply looking at them alone and isolated from circumstances. But where we see the lust of the eye causing people to miss the mark is when the things desired are thought to be able to provide that which only God can provide. To say it another way, we must guard against the objects of our desire being idolized. We are led down the wrong road if we place our hopes of happiness and joy on things. When we believe this way, we put our focus on the acquisition of things. This gets our focus off the true source of happiness and joy, which is a relationship with God and His provision of happiness and joy (fruits of the Spirit).

Only complete, utter dependence on God and His Word can bring true joy, peace, and sustained happiness. We must be careful that the things of this world do not become idols to us. Something that our eyes lust after can become an idol if we choose to accept the belief that possessing them will produce the fruits of the Spirit.

Paul writes concerning the fruits of the Spirit. Let's read what he had to say:

> But the fruit of the Spirit is love, joy, peace, longsuffering, kindness, goodness, faithfulness, gentleness, self-control. Against such there is no law. And those who are Christ's have

crucified the flesh with its passions and desires. If we live in the Spirit, let us also walk in the Spirit. Let us not become conceited, provoking one another, envying one another (Galatians 5:22-26).

The Lust of the Eye in Operation

Here is an example of one way the enemy could attack me if he wanted to destroy my family and any potential for ministry to others. The devil might lure me toward a carefree life exploring the tropical waters of the Caribbean. All that would be required for me to be deeply tempted is to offer me a large yacht, complete with crew and provisions, ready to sail around the islands. I am oversimplifying this to make a point. To be clear, you can be assured that satan would not use a Jon boat or canoe to tempt me. It would have to be beautiful to my natural eye and appealing to my mind's eye to gain my attention.

Another analogy that is fitting for this subject can be found in observing the deer hunter. If you are a hunter and want to go deer hunting, you prepare for the hunt before you leave the house. You may bring along some doe urine to lure the buck out of the woods. You might throw corn out near your tree stand to entice a curious buck to come a little closer. You will do these things for one reason: to lure the buck so you have a better chance of killing him. If you make a noise that he does not recognize, he will run. If you make sudden movements, he will run. Your job as a hunter is to hold still—almost lifeless—and blend in with your surroundings. Then, when the buck comes into range, you shoot and take him down.

This example is an excellent picture of the lust of the eye used in a destructive way. The deer is looking for a good thing. He is looking for a wife, or he is looking for a meal. No one would argue that these things are bad. We can learn from this that the potential companion or meal was not responsible for the deer's death; the hunter was responsible. It was the hunter who placed things in the path of the deer to kill him.

The Twisting of a Good Thing

The lust of the eye is the twisting of a good thing. Remember earlier, we talked about how the devil cannot create anything and that he can only pervert an existing truth. The drawing away of the eye is a perversion of an existing truth. For example, a woman's physique may be attractive to a man. She was made that way by God's own hand. The way the devil perverts this is to use her beauty against a man. Here's a real-world scenario that illustrates this point well.

A young, attractive woman works in an office with a married man who is having trouble at home. He begins to confide in her about some of his frustrations. He feels he has found someone he can talk to and begins to develop a soulish relationship with her. Unfortunately, the comfort and encouragement first offered are twisted by the enemy into something illicit. One thing leads to another, and before you know it, the husband is headed for divorce court after being caught in an adulterous affair.

The affair did not start with the thought of adultery. Instead, it began with the lust of the eye. If the co-worker had been a man, it is unlikely that the conversations would have taken place. If she had not been attractive to him, it is doubtful the conversation would have begun, and if it did, it would not have progressed very far.

Bear in mind that attractiveness is not a sin, and the woman did no wrong by working with the man in the office. The error came when the man began to share his marital problems with the young woman. The lust of the eye caused the man to desire the young woman at the office with an illusion of joy and happiness that would come through gaining her affection.

Here is another example of the lust of the eye in operation. What if a glamorous job offer comes to you, complete with benefits, higher wages, and the opportunity to do what you've always wanted to do? Do you think that could be considered a lust of the eye? You better believe it. The prospect of what that job holds for you, the things you could buy, the things you could do, and the places you could go are all tied to the lust of the eye (or what you can imagine). There is nothing wrong with a job like this, and I will be honest with you, it would be tough for me to turn it down. But truth be told, without God's approval or consent, the job could be a trap of the enemy to get you off your course and lead you down a path toward destruction.

My pastor tells the story of a job offer, much like the illustration above. He was offered a job to lead the praise and worship ministry at a large and rapidly growing church. The proposal was for more money than he had ever made in his life, and it came with a bonus. He would be allowed to travel and minister on the road as much as he had been doing before taking this new job. The offer was a dream offer of sorts—more money than ever, little commitment required, and little change demanded.

At first, my pastor's response was, *"Praise God, Jesus loves me! This is the offer we've been waiting on."* But, after some prayer and deliberation, his wife sensed that this was not God's best for them. Pastor made it clear that he did not want to hear what she had to say but decided to take it to a place of prayer. After seeking God's will concerning the opportunity, my pastor agreed that the ministry offer was not from God, and they declined the position.

Little did they know, just a short time later, that church would go through a split, and he would have been out of a job after uprooting their family to take this "dream job." God knew the end from the beginning; He knew that He had called my pastor to Panama City, Florida, where he currently pastors a vibrant, growing, and powerful church. Had this other job offer been pursued, it would have delayed or possibly destroyed the potential for starting this region-changing ministry.

The lust of the eye could have heavily influenced my pastor and potentially drawn him off course had he not been submitted to the Holy Spirit and allowed the Spirit's influence to prevail. The lust of the eye would have said, *"Look at the nice home you will be able to buy. Look at the nice car you can drive. Look at the future you will be able to secure for you and your family."* All of these things are good things, and no one could argue otherwise. However, outside of the blessing of God, these things could have been the bait that lured him out into the open field where the enemy could pick him off, destroy his future destiny, and mount him on his wall, so to speak.

Now, we've established that the lust of the eye can be used to take us down the wrong road, but what is the balance to this section of the book, you might ask?

First of all, you have to get your priorities right. You must put God first in everything you do. All things must pass through the GOD-FIRST FILTER before you even consider proceeding with your decision.

Here is *Life's Priority List*, in this order:

- God first
- Wife & children *(note this is separate and above ministry)*
- Church/ministry
- Work
- Hobbies/pleasure

If we are going to make a decision to pursue something that appeals to the eye, like many of the examples previously stated, each of those desires must pass through the above priority list.

Example Use of *Life's Priority List*

Let's look at an example of how to use this priority list. I want to buy a pleasure boat. What do I need to do to use the priority list properly?

Priority One: God first. Does the desired item violate any of God's Word, commandments, or statutes? If the answer is "yes," then you may not proceed. If the answer is "no," then you may move to priority two. In this example, there is no Bible verse that says you can't have a pleasure boat. Therefore, you can proceed to the next step.

Priority Two: Wife & children. Does this item's use build a stronger relationship with your family, or does it weaken the bonds? If the answer is that it strengthens family bonds, then you may proceed to priority three. If the answer is that it weakens connections, then you may not proceed with the purchase. In this example, the boat is a family boat to be used by the whole family. Therefore, it strengthens family bonds since we will spend quality time together.

Priority Three: Church/ministry. Does this item interfere with your ability to attend church regularly, or does it interfere with your current ministry activity? If the answer is that it interferes with either, then you may not proceed to priority four. If not, then move on to priority four. In this example, the boat's use will typically fall on holidays, Saturdays, or other days when there is spare time. We should establish a set of rules which permits the use of the boat on days only where there is no conflict with regular church attendance or ministry. The boat could be a good idea if you are responsible enough to adhere to these self-imposed rules. If not, then the boat could become destructive instead of a blessing. If it causes you to miss church regularly, the boat is an idol in your life and will not end well for you.

Priority Four: Work. Does this item interfere with your job? To say it another way, does purchasing this item interfere with your work schedule or ability to work? You can proceed to the final priority if the answer is no. If the answer is yes, then it would be best not to purchase the item because it would help you avoid potential failure at your job. It is feasible that the purchase of a boat could interfere with your work schedule if you let it. You would have to choose to use the boat when time allows. As mentioned earlier, you'd likely have time on Saturdays and holidays if you're like most people who work a full-time job.

Priority Five: Hobbies/pleasure. This item is considered at the bottom of life's priority list. It is an unnecessary item that has no bearing on your major priorities in life. This purchase would be categorized as a hobby/pleasure, and if properly prioritized, it will be a blessing to you and your family.

Keep in mind that this priority list is there to help you keep essential things in proper perspective and prevent you from falling victim to the lust of the eye. If what you desire can pass the test of life's priority list, then it will not be destructive to you or your family, and that is really the point of this chapter. This chapter was written to emphasize the potential destruction for which the lust of the eye can be responsible and help you better discern if you are being drawn by the lust of the eye.

SELFLESSNESS...
enables you to properly prioritize what is important to God and empowers you to live above the lust of the eye.

5

THE PRIDE OF LIFE

"For all that is in the world—the lust of the flesh,
the lust of the eyes, and the pride of life—is not of the
Father but is of the world" (1 John 2:16).

The phrase "the pride of life" can be interpreted in various
ways, and I am sure that if you have been saved for any
period of time, you've probably heard teaching on this
subject. Before we dive into this chapter, let's first analyze
what the pride of life is and how it is best defined.

The original Greek words for "the pride of life" are defined
this way:

> **Pride:** an impious and empty presumption
> which trusts in the stability of earthy things; an
> insolent and empty assurance, which trusts in
> its own power and resources and shamefully
> despises and violates divine laws and human
> rights (BlueLetterBible.com, Lexicon).

> **Of Life:** The period or course of life
> (BlueLetterBible.com, Lexicon).

Regarding "the pride of life," John is saying that pride causes one to look inwardly to one's self or own capabilities, thoughts, beliefs, notions, pre-dispositions, etc., acquired over the course of living their natural life. It also entails placing trust in these things instead of placing trust in the Lord. SELF is at the center of all of this.

For a practical look at this third and final trap the enemy uses, let's consider a scientist. Considered individuals of high education and intelligence, they have often studied in the best educational institutions and devoted much of their lives to understanding natural things. Astronomers will look at stars for years on end to measure their movements in relation to Earth. Molecular biologists will micro-analyze the smallest particles to see how things work. At the end of all their study, a scientist will have newfound knowledge that can be applied to natural things.

However, something else can accompany this gaining of newfound insight, and that is the pride of life or simply pride. This root of pride is identified by its actions. The educated man or woman gains learning or understanding that an uneducated person does not possess. In their minds, this can give them a reason to deem themselves superior in intellect or knowledge, or in some cases, the delusion of having supremacy in every arena of life. In reality, gaining understanding or knowledge does not make them any better or superior to any other human being. Knowledge and education merely establish that one possesses data that another person is lacking, and they have an opportunity to apply this knowledge in a way that will either benefit themselves or others. I am sure you have met someone who behaves in this manner. Can you see the nature of the enemy at work?

Satan's desire to place himself above others is demonstrated in the prideful thinking of the scientist in our example. Absent the influence of the Holy Spirit, who would guide this learned individual toward humility and grace to others? We see the signature of the enemy once again. Satan's motives and desires are for him to be above and exalted. Therefore, those who are led by their flesh (self) will act in a similar manner.

For the scientist, gaining this knowledge was not in any way sinful. On the contrary, we should all attain as much understanding of natural things as we can. Doing this will enable us to pursue new ideas, innovate products, and develop services. It also equips us to solve problems and explore new opportunities. Each of these pursuits makes the world a better place to live. The error that leads to sin is when the knowledge gained causes one to place him or herself in a place of superiority.

The pride of life, as illustrated in Genesis as the tree to "make one wise," is a two-edged sword. While wisdom is good for keeping us on the straight and narrow path, it is also an area where pride can slip in and divide you from others with whom you come in contact. The enemy's primary goal and focus is to create division, separation, discord (as the Bible calls it), and divorce, ultimately leading to destruction. These things are simply in the enemy's nature. The pride of life is found in many other areas. Let's look at another example.

Accomplishment Can Lead to Pride

Imagine a person who feels unattractive. Under the influence of the enemy, they begin to formulate negative thoughts about themselves concerning their physical appearance. They might think things like, *"No one is going to like me,"* or *"I won't find a spouse because I am not attractive,"* or *"I am going to be rejected."* These are all lies, but to stay on point, they illustrate the contrast of what happens next. Let's say this person decides to make some changes to their outward appearance. In their mind, changing their hairstyle, wearing contact lenses, exercising, or getting plastic surgery aims to improve how they see themselves. They want others to treat them how they desire to be treated. Is there anything wrong with this? No, but anything taken to an extreme is a signature of the perversion of the enemy that ultimately will lead to the pride of life.

I can personally attest to this because I was once this guy. I was scrawny and thin, but I perceived being thin negatively and wanted to see change. So, I began to work out and eat right. I exercised at least 2 hours every day, and over the course of a few years, I saw major changes in my physique. However, while the change was good, the resulting pride that accompanied the difference was not.

This pride in my life was the third example of what John wrote about, the pride of life. I was looking to my earth-suit or flesh as the source of my supposed happiness. The pride of life told me I possessed something desired by others, and since I had it, I was superior—a winner. This way of thinking has the enemy's signature written all over it. Believing this lie caused me to live my life in a manner that was similar to the way the devil conducted his life.

Absent the influence of the Holy Spirit and knowledge of Christ's words to be humble, the individual who once felt alone, rejected, and of little value starts to see change, and their opinion of themselves shifts away from *"I am ugly or worthless."* Instead, they begin to feel confident and positive about their outward appearance. This new attitude is where the pride of life can creep in. The person sees things in a whole new light; they secretly despise what they once were and now see themselves in a place of superiority to their old self.

Keep in mind that the word "sin" literally means "to miss the mark." Therefore, acting like the devil does not require that you operate in *egregious sin* because to sin is to err or to be off target. What is the target? The target for Christians is to humble oneself under the mighty hand of God and to submit oneself to serve others. This could be referred to as hitting the bull's eye. Again, the concept of sin and missing the mark is like a poorly shot arrow that misses the target. In God's eyes, all sin is bad. Using archery as an analogy, your goal is to draw back your arrow, aim true, and hit the center of the center circle on the target downrange. If you miss the bull's eye, you miss the mark.

God is not a bully, and He does not heap shame and condemnation on you when you miss the mark. Instead, He encourages you to pick up another arrow, take a deep breath, draw, sight, and shoot again. In the end, if you do this consistently, your arrows will fly straight and true, and you will accomplish the objective you set out to accomplish, being on target.

This is all that a good father will ask of his sons. He'll say listen and learn, be equipped, trained, and prepared for the task at hand. Then when you face challenges, you will be victorious over them. If you do not first succeed, try again. You will reap if you faint not. So keep trying; keep moving forward.

Now that we've exposed the pride of life, we will move on to our next subject: how to break the self-nature.

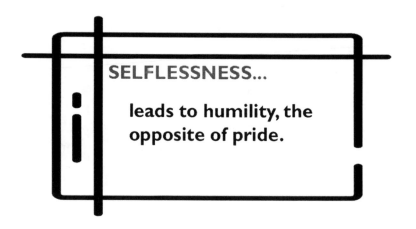

SELFLESSNESS...

leads to humility, the opposite of pride.

SECTION 3

THE SOLUTION: JESUS GIVES US THE HIDDEN ANSWER

DEATH TO SELFIE

6

Submission to the Father

In chapters 1-5, we've learned a lot about the common problem of selfishness and how it manifests in our lives. I'd like to now focus on the solution to the problem. To find the answer, we need only to find a mentor from whom we may glean wisdom and understanding on the subject.

Dr. Robert Gay teaches that if we seek success in a given area within our lives, we must first seek to find someone demonstrating success in this area and then begin to emulate their actions. For instance, if you would like to get some sound marital advice, it is a good idea to obtain it from someone who is successfully married, who has given sound marital advice to others with good results, and who has not been divorced multiple times. If you want financial advice, obtaining this information from someone with a strong credit rating and who has been successful with earnings, savings, and investments would be optimal. One would not want to seek financial advice from someone who filed for bankruptcy on multiple occasions and currently does not have a job!

This teaching is a proper application of sound wisdom, and I have applied it in my own life and have seen great rewards in many areas as a result. So, who should we seek to emulate if we desire to eradicate the SELF-nature from our lives? We should look to the most selfless person that ever lived, Jesus.

We are now going to dive into a case study on Jesus, which will be divided into two sections. The first chapter is titled "Submission to the Father," which is a critical component in learning to live a life of selflessness. The second one is titled "Selflessness Defeats Sin." During this study, we will read every instance Jesus spoke about these subjects. When complete, we should be able to glean much wisdom and understanding from the heart of Jesus and the Father concerning these two subjects. With this information, you will be equipped to move forward to the next section of this book, which deals with applying the solution in your own life.

Not My Will

If you read all the red words in a red-letter Bible, you will see that Jesus had much to say about many topics. After all, Jesus is the Word made flesh, so it is fitting that He had a lot to say. But, if you read every word that He spoke as one body of text, you will begin to see patterns and common threads in His speech. In the following Scripture references, you will see 17 passages where Jesus teaches about submission to the Father. Given that Jesus' teachings are primarily contained within the four gospels, I would say that any subject mentioned 17 times in four books is a subject to which we should pay attention. Before we dive into the study, let's look at these verses where Jesus speaks about submitting to the Father.

- While resisting the devil in the wilderness in Matthew 4, Jesus demonstrates submission to the Father three times. First, in verse 4, when He says, "It is written, 'Man shall not live by bread alone, but by every word that proceeds from the mouth of God.'" Then He says in verse 7, "It is written again, 'You shall not tempt the Lord your God.'" Finally, in verse 10, Jesus says, "Away with you, Satan! For it is written, 'You shall worship the Lord your God, and Him only shall you serve.'" In Matthew 7:21, near the end of the Sermon on the Mount, Jesus teaches that in order to enter the kingdom of heaven, one must do the will of the Father.

- While preaching the Sermon on the Mount in Matthew 5-7, in the Lord's Prayer, Jesus instructs us repeatedly to worship the Father God and desire His will to be done.

- In Matthew 7:21, near the end of the Sermon on the Mount, Jesus teaches that to enter the kingdom of heaven, one must do the will of the Father.

- In Matthew 26, while Jesus is praying in the Garden of Gethsemane, He says this to His Father: "O My Father, if it is possible, let this cup pass from Me; nevertheless, not as I will, but as You will" (v.39). Again in verse 42, Jesus prays, "O My Father, if this cup cannot pass away from Me unless I drink it, Your will be done."

- In Mark 14, Jesus is again quoted concerning the prayer in the Garden. The importance of this night is emphasized by including Jesus' prayer in Matthew and Mark. Jesus, praying to His Father, says, "Abba, Father, all things are possible for You. Take this cup away from Me; nevertheless, not what I will, but what You will" (v.36).

- In Luke 2, Jesus, even as a child, is recorded as saying, "Did you not know that I must be about my Father's business?" (v.49).

- In Luke 4, in response to three temptations of the devil, Jesus responds to each one with submission to the Father. First, Jesus says, "It is written, 'Man shall not live by bread alone, but by every word of God'" (v.4). Then He says, "Get behind me, Satan! For it is written, 'You shall worship the Lord your God, and Him only you shall serve'" (v.8). Finally, He says, "It has been said, 'You shall not tempt the Lord your God'" (v.12).

- Again, in Luke 11:2-4, we see Jesus teaching the Lord's prayer, which begins with the exhortation to praise God's name and submit to God's will.

- In Luke 22:42, Jesus is praying in the Garden of Gethsemane and says, "Father, if it is Your will, take this cup away from Me, nevertheless not My will, but Yours, be done." We see a continual echoing of the Son submitting to the will of the Father.

- In John 4:34, Jesus says, "My food is to do the will of Him who sent Me, and to finish His work."

- In John 5:19, Jesus says, "Most assuredly I say to you, the Son can do nothing of Himself, but what He sees the Father do; for whatever He does, the Son also does in like manner."

- Again, in John 5:30, Jesus says, "I can of Myself do nothing. As I hear, I judge; and My judgment is righteous, because I do not seek My own but the will of the Father who sent Me."

- In John 6:38, Jesus says, "For I have come down from heaven, not to do My own will, but the will of Him who sent Me."

- In John 8:28-29, Jesus further solidifies His submission to the Father by saying:

  When you lift up the Son of Man, then you will know that I am He, and that I do nothing of Myself; but as My Father taught Me, I speak these things. And He who sent Me is with Me. The Father has not left Me alone, for I always do those things that please Him.

- In John 12:49-50, Jesus says:

  For I have not spoken on My own authority; but the Father who sent Me gave Me a command, what I should say and what I should speak. And I know that His command is everlasting life. Therefore, whatever I speak, just as the Father had told Me, so I speak.

- In John 14:31, Jesus says, "But that the world may know that I love the Father, and as the Father gave Me commandment, so I do."

Jesus Examples Greatness on the Mountain

Now let's take a closer look at one of the most detailed accounts of Jesus' demonstration of submission to the Father. It is Jesus' handling of the attack of the enemy while He is being tempted after the 40-day fast in the wilderness:

> Then Jesus was led up by the Spirit into the wilderness to be tempted by the devil. And when He had fasted forty days and forty nights, afterward He was hungry. Now when the tempter came to Him, he said, "If You are the Son of God, command that these stones become bread." But He answered and said, "It is written, 'Man shall not live by bread alone, but by every word that proceeds from the mouth of God.'" Then the devil took Him up into the holy city, set Him on the pinnacle of the temple, and said to Him, "If You are the Son of God, throw Yourself down. For it is written: 'He shall give His angels charge over you, and, 'In their hands they shall bear you up, Lest you dash your foot against a stone.'" Jesus said to him, "It is written again, 'You shall not tempt the LORD your God.'" Again, the devil took Him up on an exceedingly high mountain, and

showed Him all the kingdoms of the world and their glory. 9 And he said to Him, "All these things I will give You if You will fall down and worship me." Then Jesus said to him, "Away with you, Satan! For it is written, 'You shall worship the LORD your God, and Him only you shall serve.'" Then the devil left Him, and behold, angels came and ministered to Him (Matthew 4:1-11).

In Matthew 4:3, the enemy attempts to lure Jesus to think of HIMSELF and His flesh using His hunger, also known as the "lust of the flesh." We must understand that chasing after our fleshly appetites can often lead to destruction. Jesus deflects the attack by coming under the mighty hand of God and saying, "Man shall not live by bread alone, but by every word that proceeds out of the mouth of God." Jesus does not think of His own need at this moment; He points away from Himself and brings the focus back to His Father. Noting His actions is of utmost importance if we are going to begin living as Jesus did. Jesus was showing us that He was submitted to the Father's will to the point that it physically hurt; this is the embodiment of selflessness. Jesus put God before Himself. We must do the same by letting God be most important in our lives.

How do we put God first? We **obey His written Word—** the Bible, and we comply with **proper spiritual authority.** To put it another way, we should read our Bibles daily to know what is inside the written Word of God. We should also apply the spoken Word of God, which our spiritual headship imparts to us. We will talk about this more in another chapter.

In the second temptation in Matthew 4:5, the devil takes Jesus up to the temple's highest point. He tells Jesus to throw Himself down and then cites a twisted version of the Scripture to get Jesus to take the bait. Jesus again demonstrates His submission to the Father by saying, "You shall not tempt the Lord your God." Jesus knew that tempting God was an attempt to put Himself in a place of equality with God. Said another way, it would have been prideful to think of Himself as equal to God. That is what we do when we question God or His Word.

Pride is exalting your own opinion above that which God has spoken. We, in essence, place our thoughts and ideas in a place of equality with His. In doing so, we are operating in pride, and in this case, it is a demonstration of the pride of life being used by the enemy to get Jesus to fail.

In verse Matthew 4:8, satan's third attack attempts to bait Jesus with power and grandeur. Satan offers Him the kingdoms of the world and their glory in exchange for Jesus bowing down to him. Satan will always try to lure you with that which ensnared him. He is so consumed with pride that it is a foregone conclusion that all exposed to his influence will undoubtedly think and act as he does. Satan once again demonstrates what is inside him by attempting to use something that he thought would appeal to Jesus' eye, also known as the lust of the eye. Satan offers the glory of this world, the authority to rule, for Jesus to possess Himself. Jesus immediately takes authority over satan, recognizing his attempt to rise up, and then sends him away. Jesus finishes it off with another indicator of where His inward motivations lie. Jesus says, "For it is written, 'You shall worship the Lord your God, and Him only shall you serve'" (Matthew 4:10b). He is saying that, once again, *"It is not about Me; it is about Him."*

The outcome of the story of Jesus' temptation on the mountain is taught in James 4:7. Jesus submitted to His Father, He resisted the devil, and the devil departed. Then James 4:10 says, "Humble yourselves in the sight of the Lord, and He will lift you up." You will see this emphasized again and again throughout this book. Submission to the Father is humility in action.

Jesus, Our Mentor

In each of the Scriptures we've just read, we can see a key theme in the life of Jesus. He came into this world as flesh and bone, just like you and me, yet He was fully God. Jesus had the ability to speak things into existence with His Word. He commanded demons to flee, called dead people back to life, multiplied food, walked on water, and the list goes on and on. The point is that while here on earth, in human form, Jesus chose to submit to His Father's will. As a man, Jesus could have chosen to disobey God's call on His life, but He did not. Jesus came to earth in the same flesh and bone that you and I possess.

Jesus' submission to the Father is so profound because He CHOSE to submit to the authority in His life. Jesus chose to get behind the vision that His Father had cast. Jesus knew proper order in both heaven and earth, and He chose to demonstrate God's order for the whole world to see on the greatest stage the world has ever known. Jesus was a doer of God's Word.

When I became a Christian, I earnestly prayed the prayer of salvation. Do you remember those words? Let me repeat one part, which typically finds its way into most salvation prayers: "Jesus, be Lord of my life, take control of my life..." If we want to make Jesus the Lord of our lives, we should do as Jesus did and be doers of His Word. Think about it.

Jesus is the best mentor anyone could ever have; He had something working in His life. Jesus performed more miracles, signs, and wonders than any minister that has ever walked the face of this earth. The Lord has more fruit in His ministry than any other pastor that has ever lived. Jesus is literally the Word of God made flesh. If we are truly serious about our faith, we should do everything in our power to mirror Jesus' every action, thought, mannerism, and even Spirit. How do we do that? We do it by getting into His Word! We do this by devouring His words like we would a filet mignon steak. Not just once, but we should do this every day of our lives. We must begin to see the words of Jesus as literal food necessary for sustenance. Then we must activate them in our lives by practicing them. This follow-through is what the Bible talks about in James when referring to "works."

Faith Without Works is Dead

One of my favorite Scriptures in all of the Bible is found in James 2:14-26. James, one of Jesus' twelve disciples and one of the three closest to Jesus, is writing concerning the difference between having faith in word only versus faith with confirming works. This passage is particularly powerful because it requires the believer to assess their faith realistically, quantifying it with a test. Do you have faith?

James says that if you do, you will have works also. Conversely, if you do not have works, you do not have faith.

Works are a byproduct of your faith. Your faith should compel you to do what you have been shown through Jesus' example. James said, "You believe that there is one God. You do well. Even the demons believe and tremble. But do you want to know, O foolish man, that faith without works is dead?" (James 2:19-20). And then, if you skip to verse 24, he finishes this line of thinking with this: "You see then that a man is justified by works, and not by faith only."

The bottom line is this: If you say you love Jesus, then you will love His Word. If you love His Word, you will submit to it and live by it. This is the "works" piece. When you live by Jesus' Word, you will have evidence or works. Jesus said:

> If anyone loves Me, he will keep My word; and My Father will love him, and We will come to him and make Our home with him. He who does not love Me does not keep My words; and the word which you hear is not Mine but the Father's who sent Me (John 14:23-24).

I want you to stop reading for a moment and ask yourself: Do I love Jesus? Do I love His Word? Am I applying His Word in my life? If you answered "yes" to all three questions, then you actually "love" Jesus. If you cannot honestly answer all three questions with a confident "yes," then there is a deficiency in your love for Jesus. If you find deficiencies in your love for the Lord, you have just discovered that change is needed. You should rejoice that you are now aware of an area in your life that needs adjustment, and now you can begin to take steps toward turning that "no" into a "yes"!

I encourage you to make a fresh heart-commitment to be obedient to every biblical command. Allow the Lord Jesus to lead and guide you in the path of life. Choose to prioritize your relationship with Him above all others. As you do these things, your love for Him will grow, and you will be empowered to crucify your flesh and be led by the Spirit.

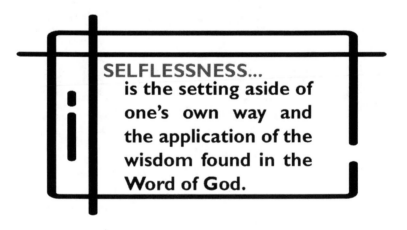

SELFLESSNESS...
is the setting aside of one's own way and the application of the wisdom found in the Word of God.

7

SELFLESSNESS DEFEATS SIN

As the name of this chapter implies, we're now going to turn our attention to Jesus' greatest strength. We will focus on an element of His character that is evident for all to see yet can only be fully appreciated when revealed by the Father. Even though we are studying this truth, I challenge you to ask the Father to reveal it through His Spirit. If we ask Him to show us and remain steadfast to stay the course, He will fully open our eyes to this truth. The simplicity of Jesus' most powerful attribute is astounding: His selflessness.

The Hidden Secret Revealed

If you only read one section in this book, this is the section you want to read. This section bears the most impact on the subject of selfless living and most plainly exposes self-nature in action. At the same time, this portion reveals to us the hidden secret of the gospel, which is selflessness!

> Now there was also a dispute among them, as to which of them should be considered the greatest. And He said to them, "The kings of the Gentiles exercise lordship over them, and

those who exercise authority over them are called 'benefactors.' But not so among you; on the contrary, he who is greatest among you, let him be as the younger, and he who governs as he who serves. For who is greater, he who sits at the table, or he who serves? Is it not he who sits at the table? Yet I am among you as the One who serves" (Luke 22:24-27).

In this passage, we read that Jesus was walking with His disciples, and an argument breaks out. Jesus overhears them selfishly debating which of them was to be considered greatest in the kingdom of heaven! I read this and thought, *"These guys really don't get it! You're walking with the very Son of God, and all you have to think about is yourself?"* Can you see the enemy's influence manifesting in these followers of Christ? Each of them wanted to see themselves lifted up above the other. Does this sound familiar? Do you remember the case study on satan? What did he do that got him kicked out of heaven? Satan was thrown out of heaven because he sought to lift himself above everyone else, including God.

Jesus, knowing their motivations during this quarrel, quotes the most powerful words, in my opinion, in the whole Bible. Therefore, I recommend you commit this passage to memory:

"For who is greater, he who sits at the table, or he who serves? Is it not he who sits at the table? Yet I am among you as the One who serves" (Luke 22:27).

Jesus gives us the hidden secret to achieving everything we could ever desire in this one passage of Scripture. Can you see it? Jesus just gave us the answer to the question on the test! In plain sight, He hid the secret many have missed since sin first entered the world. Jesus plainly says that to be great is to be least—to be great, we must serve. He goes on to say, *"I am God, and I am serving you!"* WOW! God in the flesh is serving these self-absorbed disciples and must remind them that He is God and not interested in the human perspective of greatness. Lovingly, He teaches them that selflessness and service are the answer.

This teaching aligns with Jesus' declaration in Matthew 22:39, where He says, "You shall love your neighbor as yourself." In this passage, Jesus has just responded to the scribes and Pharisees concerning their question about the "Great Commandment" in the Law. Jesus paraphrases the Ten Commandments and condenses them down into two commandments. The first is to love God; the second is to love your neighbor. When you choose to regard your neighbor as you would yourself, you are basically acknowledging that they are valuable to you, and you are making a choice to respect them and treat them well. These things are the heart of service.

But if it is this simple, why do so many miss it? I believe it is because most people allow the enemy to be the greatest influence. However, if we allow the Holy Spirit to be the most significant influence in our lives, then it is totally possible to apply this revelation successfully.

In the Presence of Greatness

Over the years, I have met many men and women who have chosen to serve others. Each possessed something similar—something real and tangible yet unseen and invisible. On each occasion with them, I felt a desire for the attributes which I observed in operation within their lives. There was greatness "oozing" from their presence. All I could do in each of these encounters was hope that one day such a wonderful thing could be found in me. It was glorious.

Even as I write this book, I am learning more and more about how to serve. The more I do it, the more I am drawn to it. It is amazing to watch how others respond to acts of service. Seeing what happens in the eyes of those who have just been shown love through service is breathtaking. Imagine a life lived in devotion to service! How rewarding it would be to serve as many as possible during your days on the earth! Imagine the wonderful reward that awaits in eternity!

Selflessness Calls Others to a Higher Level

A great example of selflessness in action was seen recently at a local prison where a friend of mine, David, works as a security guard. When David was making his rounds through the dormitory, one of the inmates was cursing as David walked by. The inmate was asked to please refrain from cursing and swearing, a common policy among the security guards. When the inmate, a rather large and burly man, stood up, pushed out his chest, and cursed again, David was caught in the middle of the age-old battle between self-nature and selflessness. The self-nature will always seek to be on top or in a place of advantage. The inmate was looking to show his fellow inmates that he was in charge of this situation and was not going to be told what to do by an authority figure.

Selflessness is what came next through a man of God who was obedient to Jesus' instructions that we should become a servant of all. David walked over to the man, and with the love of Christ shining in all its glory, he replied, "You're smart; you're intelligent, and you can do better than that." Since that day, the relationship between David and that inmate has been much different, and there is no more cursing. David called out to the man's potential by becoming low and pushing the inmate upward. This example describes selflessness in action!

The methods of Christ always speak with words of edification, exhortation, and comfort. The heart of a good Father will look at His son and say, *"Son, I created you, and I know your potential. Come up here."* Satan's response to a similar situation is to heap condemnation on someone so that he can stand on top of them.

The story of David and the inmate was shared to show you the opposite of self-nature and to draw a contrast to self-nature's way of doing things. Think about it for a minute. If you were in a situation where you were attempting to bring change to someone's life, what would you do? What would you do if you knew everything they were doing incorrectly and where they were missing it? I recommend we all do the same thing David did and exercise selflessness.

Jesus' Words are the Spirit of Prophecy

I attend a church where we have the privilege of having a pastor who not only preaches well but also operates in the gift of prophecy. Pastor Robert Gay has been prophesying for many years and has remained steady in his approach to ministry. On many occasions, he has called someone out during a worship service and prophesied the Word of the Lord to them. In every instance, the word has come forth as an encouragement to come higher. Each and every prophetic word that I have witnessed has demonstrated the love of the Father by empowering someone to look to come higher. This calling to a higher place has brought forth fruit in the lives of many people, often completely revolutionizing their lives.

The majority of Christians today would have done the opposite of what Pastor Robert or David did. In David's situation, they might have said something like, "I'm in charge here, and you will listen to me because I'm wearing the badge." Many pastors might have called a meeting with a young man who received a prophecy during the praise service. The pastor may have called it "counsel" and told the young man everything wrong in his life and used the Bible to show where he was wrong. These actions are the self-nature at work. It is evidence of how the scribes and Pharisees could have been so ignorant about the coming of Christ. They, just like this example, were so caught up in the rules of the Bible that they missed the heart of the Father in the middle of it. Instead, they allowed the influence of the enemy to be the prevailing influence in their lives.

The young man called into the office by his pastor knew precisely where he was missing it; he did not need to be told how wrong he was. Rather, he needed to hear that he could do better. Although there will always be a need for pastors to confront poor behavior, pastors must minister from a heart of restoration instead of condemnation. To seek to restore someone to proper order and right standing with God is, in fact, an act of selflessness. Lifting up someone else demonstrates a heart conviction that desires to get beneath someone else to help them reach their destiny. Can you see the simplicity of the gospel in this?

Encouragement Defeats Condemnation

Truth be told, the scribes and Pharisees could not have another spiritual influence during their time. They possessed God's Word but had not yet been given the Holy Spirit. The wonderful news is that you have been given the opportunity to receive the Holy Spirit, so you can operate with the same Holy influence present in your life as Jesus did when He was here on earth. Jesus did not come to Earth to exemplify perfection and then leave us powerless to do the same. Jesus came to earth to show us how to be just like Him. He came, broke sin's power, and then restored to us the capability to commune with the Father through His Holy Spirit. His Spirit will encourage you to look outwardly, loving others as yourself.

Many unbelievers have communicated a dislike for being around Christians because they constantly point out their sins. Relating to people this way pushes others away. If I am doing wrong, I know it. The only thing that will cause me or any other person to look in another direction is something better being offered. The truth is that you will always attract more flies with honey than with vinegar. Speaking hope and edification is a more sure means of seeing change manifested in their lives.

How would you respond to these two statements if you were an alcoholic?

1. *"Your drinking is not acceptable, and you are sinning."*
2. *"You have a purpose and destiny on your life that is currently in a holding pattern until you decide to give up alcohol."*

If I am drinking heavily, it probably has a root in some area where there is pain, and I am seeking an escape. I already know in my heart that I am doing wrong. Telling me that I am wrong only causes me to retaliate by putting up walls of defense. But, telling me that my purpose and destiny are being delayed tells me that when I put down the bottle, something greater stands ready for me. This is the way of truth and the selflessness that contradicts the self-nature.

If a man cheats on his spouse, he will likely try to cover it up. Set aside the moral wrong that adultery represents for a moment. Instead, let's look at the fact that if he gets caught cheating, his wife or girlfriend will most likely leave him. That fact in itself tells a man that he is doing wrong. Even a man without Bible knowledge still knows right from wrong in most cases. What he doesn't need at that moment is for someone operating in a self-motivated way to approach him and say, *"You're sinning, and you need to 'turn or burn.'"*

Although the Bible tells us that we need to intervene when we see our brothers and sisters going down the wrong road, we must understand that the love of Christ is going to get beneath them and push them higher, not stand on top of them and push them down lower. In this situation, Jesus would tell you the same thing he told the woman caught in adultery. He commanded her to go and sin no more; He would not throw a stone at her. Jesus had the power and authority to forgive her sin, and His selfless act caused her heart to change. She saw hope through His act of forgiveness, and that is what was needed to soften her hardened heart.

The religious leaders wanted blood in the streets. They operated in the self-nature, which wanted to be in a place of advantage. They wanted to show the woman, *"We're up here, and you're down there; now you're going to pay."* Love for the woman was demonstrated by the mercy and grace given by Jesus. Jesus did not say, *"Go and try not to do this again."* He said, "Go and sin no more." The law said that the sin of adultery was punishable by death. But what did Jesus come to do? He did not come to destroy; Jesus came to save!

Eternal Perspective

Everything we do during this life should be done through the lens or perspective of eternity. Nothing in this life will go with us when we pass—no possessions, no worldly accomplishments, no accolades or praise. All we'll have when we move on will be our actions while we were here, and we'll have to give an account to God. What a wonderful thought to know that when we get to meet Him, we won't have to worry about passing the exam! We won't have to worry about shame or failure. What if we could stand there boldly in front of our Creator and know in our very innermost being that we did everything we could while on the earth to serve Him, God the Father, just as Jesus demonstrated?

If we can't see that Jesus came as the prototype from which all of us are to be crafted and that we must, in turn, follow His lead, then we must go back and reexamine our faith. It is the belief of this author that to best honor Jesus and His selfless act of dying on that cross for us, we should replicate His every action—the big and the small. We must make it our highest priority in life to seek to be conformed to His likeness. The best way we can demonstrate our conformity to His likeness is by obeying His Word and duplicating His actions through service to others!

Jesus' Words Concerning Serving Others

Jesus had much to say on the subject of serving others. He is quoted in the Bible 26 times, speaking on the subject of living our lives selflessly with a heart to serve. Let's read a few of them so that we may set the foundation for where this chapter is heading.

- In Matthew 20:26b-28, Jesus teaches:

    "Whoever desires to become great among you, let him be your servant. And whoever desires to be first among you, let him be your slave - just as the Son of Man did not come to be served, but to serve, and to give His life a ransom for many."

- In Luke 14:7-11, Jesus teaches the importance of remaining humble. The passage ends with verse 11, where Jesus says, "For whoever exalts himself will be humbled, and he who humbles himself will be exalted."

- Again in Luke 22:24-27, we see the disciples debating who will be the greatest in the kingdom of God. Jesus says:

> "The kings of the gentiles exercise lordship over them, and those who exercise authority over them are called 'benefactors.' But not so among you; on the contrary, he who is greatest among you, let him be as the younger, and he who governs as he who serves. For who is greater, he who sits at the table, or he who serves? Is it not he who sits at the table? Yet I am among you as the One who serves" (Luke 22:25-27).

- In John 13:12-17, Jesus has just washed the feet of His disciples. He sits down and says:

> "Do you know what I have done to you? You call Me Teacher and Lord, and you say well, for so I am. If I then, your Lord and Teacher, have washed your feet, you also ought to wash one another's feet. For I have given you an example, that you should do as I have done to you. Most assuredly, I say to you, a servant is not greater than his master; nor is he who is sent greater than he who sent him. If you know these things, blessed are you if you do them."

The Greatest Act of Selflessness Ever Recorded

> And as Moses lifted up the serpent in the
> wilderness, even so must the Son of Man be
> lifted up, that whoever believes in Him should
> not perish but have eternal life (John 3:14-15).

In the passage above, Jesus speaks about something of
particular importance to this writing. Recounting the story
from the book of Numbers, Jesus refers to the staff of
Moses and the serpents that were affixed to it. Let's read
that story now to gain the context of what Jesus was
teaching:

> Then they journeyed from Mount Hor by the
> Way of the Red Sea, to go around the land of
> Edom; and the soul of the people became very
> discouraged on the way. And the people spoke
> against God and against Moses: "Why have you
> brought us up out of Egypt to die in the
> wilderness? For there is no food and no water,
> and our soul loathes this worthless bread." So
> the Lord sent fiery serpents among the people,
> and they bit the people; and many of the people
> of Israel died. Therefore the people came to
> Moses, and said, "We have sinned, for we have
> spoken against the Lord and against you; pray
> to the Lord that He take away the serpents from
> us." So Moses prayed for the people. Then the
> Lord said to Moses, "Make a fiery serpent, and
> set it on a pole; and it shall be that everyone who
> is bitten, when he looks at it, shall live." So

Moses made a bronze serpent, and put it on a pole; and so it was, if a serpent had bitten anyone, when he looked at the bronze serpent, he lived (Numbers 21:4-9).

In John 3, Jesus reveals this story is a type and symbol of His own crucifixion. It is possibly one of the most significant stories in all the Bible because it demonstrates what it takes to eradicate the power of sin and death. Jesus' act on the cross is quite simply the greatest example of selflessness ever recorded in human history. In this, we can see that selflessness crushed sin and death! Jesus' willingness to endure the most cruel and agonizing death is the ultimate selfless act. He respected the wishes of His Father and was willing to serve humanity regardless of the pain He suffered.

Isn't it fitting that this most selfless act would also destroy the power of sin, death, hell, and the grave? Selflessness defeated sin.

Becoming a Little Christ

Though the word "Christian" is often used, we sometimes lose the impact of what the word was originally created to convey. In the days following Jesus' ascension, the followers of Jesus were considered followers of Christ. These followers were close to Jesus while He was here on the earth. They knew His mannerisms; they knew His heart when He ministered. They had ringside seats to observe His every move while He ministered throughout the region. After Jesus' departure, these followers received the name "Christian," which means "little Christ."

These believers were not your average, run-of-the-mill, Sunday-only "Christians" that we either know or have been at some point in our faith walk. Instead, these believers were literally replicating Jesus' actions, mannerisms, behavior, and more. They did what God intended for every believer: walk in the Spirit just as Jesus did. This was the major lesson God wanted to teach us; He wanted us to get hold of the greatness that comes from walking in the Spirit. God knew that if His people could function as Jesus did, then the kingdom of God would be established in the earth.

People who walk daily in the Spirit can be trusted with much responsibility. They are dependable to obey. People that walk daily in the Spirit don't have an agenda; they are not cunning or manipulative. People who walk daily in the Spirit are motivated by something that is not of this world. These doers of Jesus' words are those who rise above the flesh-nature's tendency to place self over another. They subdue the flesh by choosing to give ear to a greater influence, the Holy Spirit.

I want to encourage you today that you have the same ability to choose to live your life above sin, just like Jesus did. You have been given the tools necessary to do so. Jesus defeated sin for you and sent the Holy Spirit to live in you. Now what you must do is trust that He was telling you the truth and begin to place a demand on those words by walking them out.

A Life of Selflessness

If we value Jesus' words and actions, we'll seek to replicate them in our own lives. One of the most profound ways we can emulate Jesus is to live a life of selflessness. What does that look like, you might ask?

Selflessness seeks to position "self" beneath someone else and press them upward. This is the key to greatness, according to Jesus. In heaven, greatness is measured by how you served while on Earth, not by how many served you. Selflessness will cause you to live as a giver. This does not mean allowing yourself to become someone else's doormat and permitting people to walk all over you without protecting your health and wellness. It means that you live your life with an attitude of giving to others so they will see an example of Christ's life in you. If we can do that, we will achieve the true title of Christian.

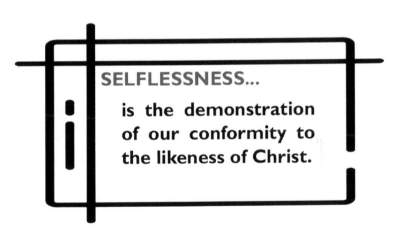

SELFLESSNESS... is the demonstration of our conformity to the likeness of Christ.

DEATH TO SELFIE

SECTION
4

APPLICATION OF THE SOLUTION: WALKING DAILY IN THE SPIRIT

DEATH TO SELFIE

8

STEP 1:
THE WORD OF GOD

I say then: Walk in the Spirit, and you shall not fulfill the lust of the flesh. For the flesh lusts against the Spirit, and the Spirit against the flesh; and these are contrary to one another, so that you do not do the things that you wish. But if you are led by the Spirit, you are not under the law. Now the works of the flesh are evident, which are: adultery, fornication, uncleanness, lewdness, idolatry, sorcery, hatred, contentions, jealousies, outbursts of wrath, selfish ambitions, dissensions, heresies, envy, murders, drunkenness, revelries, and the like; of which I tell you beforehand, just as I also told you in time past, that those who practice such things will not inherit the kingdom of God. But the fruit of the Spirit is love, joy, peace, longsuffering, kindness, goodness, faithfulness, gentleness, self-control. Against such there is no law. And those who are Christ's have crucified the flesh with its passions and desires. If we live in the Spirit, let us also walk in the Spirit. Let us not become conceited, provoking one another, envying one another (Galatians 5:16-26).

Walking in the Spirit

In his letter to the Galatians, Paul wrote about a topic many have heard, but not all have received a revelation as to what this means. The subject is how to walk in the Spirit.

When I was a young Christian, I read this and was unclear as to what it meant and how to apply this teaching in my life. I could not comprehend the concept of walking in a spiritual way. I was like Nicodemus when Jesus talked to him about being born again. I was taking the term literally and could not see with the eyes of the spirit.

During the course of writing this book, the Lord began to deal with me on what it means to "walk in the Spirit." Put simply, walking in the spirit is to live with the Holy Spirit being the chief influence in your life. Your actions are wholly dictated by biblical instruction, godly counsel, and the urging of the Spirit. When you walk in the Spirit, you choose to die to your flesh, which we've learned is your self-nature responding to the enemy's influence. When you choose to die to your flesh, you put those things that are of the enemy to death. You choose to live above those things. If you study Galatians 5:19-21, you'll see all sorts of sins listed. Selfish ambition is right in the middle of all these egregious sins. Interestingly, selfish ambition can be traced back to the roots of each of these sins.

Conversely, in Galatians 5:22, Paul writes about the fruits of the Spirit: love, joy, peace, longsuffering, kindness, goodness, faithfulness, gentleness, and self-control. He then says that those who are Christ's have crucified the flesh with its passions and desires. This passage means that if you are a Christian, you should see these nine things manifesting in your life. If the Holy Spirit is permitted to be the greatest influence in your life, then these fruits will hang from your branches. Do not be dismayed if you do not observe these fruits in your life. Instead, be encouraged that you can develop that fruit beginning now.

Let me share a lesson the Lord taught me that has helped me test whether I am walking in the Spirit. It is simple and can be applied by asking yourself three questions. I call it the *Walking in the Spirit Survey.*

1. Is my current action or thought in alignment with the Word of God?
2. Is my current action or thought in alignment with the leading of the Holy Spirit?
3. Is my current action or thought in alignment with instruction given by spiritual authority?

Once you have asked yourself these three questions, if you can say yes to each, you are indeed walking in the spirit. If you think you're hearing from the Holy Spirit, but it doesn't line up with Scripture or your spiritual authority, you must ignore what you heard. God's Word, the voice of the Holy Spirit, and proper spiritual authority in your life should always be in agreement. To be sure you're walking in the Spirit, you must ensure that all three questions are answered in the affirmative; not one may be in dissent. In this agreement, there is safety, and you will adhere to a much higher standard. Now that we've laid the groundwork for walking in the Spirit, let's turn to the first question in the test.

Question 1: Are My Actions in Alignment with the Word of God?

Romans tells us:

> And do not be conformed to this world, but be transformed by the renewing of your mind, that you may prove what is that good and acceptable and perfect will of God (Romans 12:2).

Renewing Your Mind

To renew your mind, or to say it another way, to modify your thinking, you must first establish a solid foundation on which you can plant your thought processes. When a builder builds a home, before doors are hung and walls are built, there is a building plan and a site plan. This plan always begins the building process with the building's foundation. If this foundation is built correctly, the house may stand indefinitely. If the foundation is not constructed accurately, the building cannot stand, for the foundation is the strength of the house.

We see in Ephesians 2:20 that the Church and its foundation are compared directly to a builder laying the foundation of a building. Further, Paul writes that Jesus is the chief cornerstone. Therefore, it is of utmost importance that we understand the meaning of a cornerstone. The cornerstone is the first stone laid for a masonry building's foundation. The cornerstone is vital as every other stone will be set in reference to this stone, thus determining the structure's location and orientation.

We also see in John 1:1-2 where John, the disciple that Jesus loved, writes, "In the beginning was the **Word** and the **Word** was with God and the **Word** was God. He was in the beginning with God" (emphasis added). He, being Jesus, was with God in the beginning. Jesus was, is, and will be the Word forever; He is the cornerstone of the Church. Jesus is the principal stone that was laid so that the rest of the structure may have its reference and pull its strength from that stone.

So, to transform our minds and see our minds appropriately renewed, we must look to the Word! We must look to Jesus. We must not only look to the words in red, which are essential in the life of a believer, but we must also look to every other part of the Word of God from Genesis 1 to Revelation 22. The entire Word of God is for us all—every page, every passage, and every verse. It is our responsibility to become students of the Word to such a degree that we begin to see it reconciled to itself. In other words, we must seek to study the Word so that God pours out revelation to us that enables us to tie the entirety of the Word together, being in harmony with itself.

Many people have attempted to disprove portions of the Bible or even rewrite entire sections of it because they felt that the Word was in conflict with itself. No single human being is qualified to rewrite Scripture. The Bible clearly states that all Scripture was inspired by God and is profitable for doctrine, reproof, correction, and instruction in righteousness (1 Timothy 3:16).

Some Christian leaders today preach a message that somehow separates the Old Testament from the New

Testament as if God was different in the Old Testament than from how He is today. My Bible says that Jesus is the same yesterday, today, and forevermore. Jesus is the Word! He is unchanging in both the Old and New Testament, and He is still alive today and forever. In Malachi 3:6, God says, "For I am the Lord, I do not change." The apostle James said that God has no variation or shadow of turning.

We cannot choose a path that leads us to accept that God's Word is a restaurant buffet where we pick and choose which parts to believe. Instead, we must decide to be submitted to Him and the entirety of His Word, allowing His Word to transform our lives foundationally.

We have established that a foundation must be laid, and this foundation must be the Bible. What do you suppose God would want you to use as your most basic building blocks when establishing your spiritual foundation?

The Greatest Commandments

To quote Dr. Robert Gay, we should choose God's "top ten" list as our first priority when setting the foundation of our spiritual lives. Not only did Dr. Gay say this, but Jesus Himself said it. In Matthew 19:16-19, Jesus very plainly states that in order to receive eternal life, you must keep the Commandments. If this is unclear, you should read on as Jesus begins to list many of the Commandments for the man to whom He is speaking. In another instance, a Pharisee asks Jesus which is the Great Commandment, and He responds in an interesting way:

> Jesus said to him, "'You shall love the Lord your
> God with all your heart, with all your soul, and
> with all your mind.' This is the first and great
> commandment. And the second is like it: 'You
> shall love your neighbor as yourself.' On these
> two hang all the Law and the Prophets"
> (Matthew 22:37-40).

During Jesus' day, the law and the prophets were another
way of saying "The Bible." The Bible was the Torah, the
first five books of the Bible that we have today, or the books
of Moses. The remaining books were classified as "the
prophets."

Jesus' wise response to the scribes and Pharisees answered
which Commandment was greatest by saying that all of
them are great and all should be revered as such. He was
even so bold as to say that all of the Bible, as they knew it,
hung on these two commandments! Wow!

The interesting thing about Jesus' reply to the scribes and
Pharisees in Matthew 22 is that the two commandments
He mentions are not precisely articulated in the way we
read them in the Old Testament. Actually, they are not
written that way at all. Jesus wisely summarizes the first
four commandments into His first statement, "You shall
love the Lord your God with all your heart, with all your
soul, and with all your mind" (Matthew 22:37), which is
another way of saying, "Honor God." Each of the first four
commandments is in direct correlation to honoring God.
Then, when Jesus says to "love your neighbor as yourself."

This directly correlates to the remaining six commandments, which are focused on honoring your neighbor (mother, father, brothers, sisters, family, friends, and even those with whom you're not in covenant).

With humility, we must accept Jesus' teaching by going back to the beginning to set a solid foundation upon which we may handle the load the Lord wants to place upon us. We must establish a foundation upon the Word of God! If Jesus said it, that settles it.

Let's look at the Ten Commandments in Exodus 20 so that we have a quick reference for the entire list:

- Commandment 1: "You shall have no other gods before Me."

- Commandment 2: "You shall not make for yourself a carved image—any likeness of anything that is in heaven above, or that is in the earth beneath, or that is in the water under the earth; you shall not bow down to them nor serve them."

- Commandment 3: "You shall not take the name of the LORD your God in vain..."

- Commandment 4: "Remember the Sabbath day, to keep it holy."

- Commandment 5: "Honor your father and your mother..."

- Commandment 6: "You shall not murder."

- Commandment 7: "You shall not commit adultery."

- Commandment 8: "You shall not steal."

- Commandment 9: "You shall not bear false witness against your neighbor."

- Commandment 10: "You shall not covet your neighbor's house; you shall not covet your neighbor's wife, nor his male servant, nor his female servant, nor his ox, nor his donkey, nor anything that is your neighbor's."

Each of the above-listed commandments is an instance of God's top ten list. When God had the opportunity to write the things that were on His mind and give them to His people, don't you think that He chose the ten most important things? Jesus literally said that upon the Commandments hung the entire law and the prophets. That is saying a lot. Jesus tells us that prioritizing the Ten Commandments will cause us to better understand the entire Word of God!

So where do we go from here? We understand that the Ten Commandments are good, and we should obey them. Now what? The next thing we need to do is to get an understanding of the heart behind the Commandments. Said another way, we must begin to seek out the "why" behind the Commandments and how they relate to us as new covenant believers.

This concept was brought to my attention while reading the book *Next Level: Raising the Standard of Grace* (Parsons Publishing House, 2013). In his book, Dr. Robert Gay dissects the Ten Commandments one by one, highlighting their use in the Old Testament and then illustrating how each is rearticulated in the New Testament by Jesus, Paul, and others. He then shows that these commandments call us to a higher level of responsibility and covenant with the Father and place on us a higher level of faith in Him. In this, we can begin to see the heart of the Father—His Spirit or intention behind the Commandments.

You Shall Not Murder

Dr. Robert Gay has this to say in his book:

> The first thing I want to point out is the overarching principle that we see taking place. Jesus takes the commandment "thou shall not murder" to the next level. He raises the standard and explains the heart of the Father within the commandment. Jesus points out that the commandment is more than refraining from killing someone... Jesus addresses that which is at the root of anger and murder, which is offense and unforgiveness. He (Jesus) begins to deal with the process of handling offense.

If we're going to die to our self-nature successfully, we must do as Jesus did and walk daily in the Spirit. To do this, we need a firm understanding of the Word of God, just as Jesus did. Having a solid understanding of the Bible means that we don't just read the "what" of the Word but attain the "why" of the Word. The quote from *Next Level* concerning the root of murder being offense and unforgiveness indicates we should begin to rid ourselves of any of those issues we may be holding. We choose to let go of these seemingly inconsequential seeds to keep them from maturing into hard-to-remove roots that lead to actions as severe as murder. Selfishness seeks to hold on to hurts and offenses. Selflessness lets go of those hurts and forgives. Choosing to forgive is a truly selfless act, which is acting like Jesus.

You Shall Not Commit Adultery

In this passage, Jesus had just been speaking to those attending the Sermon on the Mount. Jesus told them:

> "You have heard that it was said to those of old, 'You Shall Not Commit Adultery.' But I say to you that whoever looks at a woman to lust for her has already committed adultery with her in his heart. If your right eye causes you to sin, pluck it out and cast it from you; for it is more profitable for you that one of your members perish, than for your whole body to be cast into hell. Furthermore it has been said 'Whoever divorces his wife, let him give her a certificate of divorce.' But I say that whoever divorces his wife for any reason except sexual immorality causes her to commit adultery; and whoever marries a woman who is divorced commits adultery" (Matthew 5:27-32).

In *Next Level*, Dr. Gay expounds:

> The fact that Jesus begins to talk about divorce
> in relation to adultery reveals that He is
> expounding on the heart of the commandment.
> The heart of the commandment involves the
> issues of covenant and commitment. The fact is
> that adultery and divorce are the end result of
> covenant breaking. Adultery and divorce are the
> result of commitments being annulled.
>
> Jesus connected lust, adultery, and divorce
> together. He revealed that these are the result
> of the breaking of covenant and commitment.
> This is the heart of the commandment. Keep
> the covenants and the commitments that you
> make.

Jesus explains that God's original intent was for us to avoid
adultery but also how we could live a life of blessing. Jesus
is saying that if you're looking at a person who is not your
spouse in a way that causes you to desire them sexually, stop
it now, and it won't mature. Stop it now, and it won't cost
your marriage. Stop it now, and it won't destroy you. Can
you see it? The next level is a higher standard; the New
Testament is a higher standard. Same God! Higher
Standard!

What I love about this teaching is that Jesus' words are
given the true honor they deserve. Jesus' words were to give
honor back to the Father and give His people revelation
about what the Father intended when He first wrote the
command. Jesus gives us the inside scoop on what God was
saying all along.

We clearly see where Jesus takes the Word of God and launches it to a whole new level. Only Jesus could do this, for He knew the Father and the Father's intent when He first penned the command. With this knowledge and revelation of the power of Jesus' teaching, words in red now evoke a new level of excitement each time I read them. They are instructions from the very Son of God—not only instructions but insight into the very heart of our Creator! If we can truly get this—stop questioning Jesus, stop questioning God, and just get on board with what He said—do you think we might see some blessing on the other side? The answer is YES!

Jesus was saying this as He preached that day at the Sermon on the Mount. His beginning word was "Blessed." He said this many times throughout His teaching. Jesus wanted to see His people blessed just as He wants to see you blessed. By following Jesus' revelatory teaching, we can put into practice the very motivations of God's heart into our lives and begin living our lives as Jesus did, above sin and corruption, in the fullness of what God intended us to be.

Receiving Jesus for Who He Is

John 1:1 says, "In the beginning was the Word and the Word was with God and the Word was God. He was in the beginning with God." Notice that "Word" is capitalized; "the Word" is Jesus. "He" is Jesus. We must see Jesus literally as the Bible in the flesh. Once we get this revelation, reading the words in red becomes much more interesting. Wow, what a privilege!

The words of Jesus should take you from a place of merely reading the Commandments or reading your Bible to a place of understanding why they were written. Here is an analogy I like to use that helps me grasp how God saw mankind when He wrote the Old Testament.

Imagine a father that has a son who is two years old. His son is walking with him one day, and they approach a busy street with cars buzzing by at a high rate of speed. The son darts out, running for the road, and the father reacts with a shout and grabs his son by the arm to pull him back. There is little discussion at this point about the dangers of cars and how they could potentially cause injury. The son is simply too young to understand. This analogy is a picture of what God saw in us, His children, when He wrote the Old Testament.

The New Testament is not completely different from the Old Testament. However, it is a higher standard with higher promises written to a maturing body of believers who now have Jesus, God's Son. Jesus came to shed light on the Spirit of the author, our Heavenly Father.

Jesus' words are revelation—insight into the Scriptures. His words explain much of what is written in the Old Testament. Jesus said:

> Do not think that I came to destroy the Law or the Prophets. I did not come to destroy but to fulfill. Do not think that I came to destroy the Law or the Prophets. I did not come to destroy but to fulfill (Matthew 5:17).

Jesus was here to shine the light on all Scripture and to open our eyes to what the Lord wanted to do with each of us. He did not come to bring a new thing; He did not come with a different teaching or to replace old doctrine. Instead, Jesus came with a message that empowered God's people to live free from the bondage of sin and death and begin living in the fullness of God's purpose for them. Jesus came with "the why" behind the commandments, just like a father who brings understanding to a mature son.

For example, when the woman was caught in adultery, and the religious leaders cried out for her to be stoned, what did Jesus do? He tells her to go and sin no more. He gives her a direct commandment, not only to obey the Bible but never do it again. "Sin no more" is certainly a higher level than many of us aspire to achieve.

Words in Red

When you read your Bible, many print versions will have the words of Jesus printed in red. If you're reading the Bible on your phone or tablet or on a web-based Bible site like *Bible Gateway*, you can select "words in red" in the settings menu, and Jesus' words will appear in red, while all the other text appears in black.

I recently took the time to read every red word in the Bible, all within a few days. My simple purpose was to document every instance of Jesus speaking on the subject matter of this book. I felt it was better to read every word than to trust keyword searches, which could potentially miss an important truth. Something interesting happened when I read only the words in red; I felt something I had never felt before. I felt stronger in my faith and fuller in my spirit. It was like I had just eaten a four-course meal full of carbs and protein. Then, I was reminded of the words Jesus spoke when He said, "The words that I speak to you are Spirit, and they are life" (John 6: 63). After reading every word in red, I felt full, like Jesus' words were literal food.

The Example of Jesus

To be a Christian is defined to be "a little Christ." That is what it means when you're genuinely demonstrating Christian behavior. When Christ ascended to heaven, His followers were left behind and acted as Jesus did. As a result, people said things like, "There goes one of those followers of Christ." Eventually, Christian, or little Christ, became the simplest word to convey that title, and it stuck.

Christians should seek to emulate Jesus' every behavior. We are not only commanded to do so but also enabled to do so. The Bible says Jesus became the firstborn of many brethren (Romans 8:29), meaning that we, as sons of God, have the same power through the Holy Spirit that Jesus had while He walked the earth.

The Bible also says, "I can do all things through Christ who strengthens me" (Philippians 4:13). Remember the reference to the foundation upon which our spiritual house is built? Jesus is the chief cornerstone and the very first thing our foundation is built upon. He sets the direction of our spiritual house, and He is the strength of that house. No house is any stronger than the foundation upon which it is laid. If Jesus is our foundation, then we can be sure that our spiritual house will stand regardless of the storms that may come.

To better understand Jesus and the example He was to His disciples, I began to study each of the four gospels together, reading them at the same time and looking for things that Jesus did consistently. I was looking for His mannerisms and indicators of His heart or inward motivations. This study was particularly eye-opening and of great value to me.

Christian

As we said, to be a Christian is to be a little Christ. To be a little Christ is to look like Jesus, act like Jesus, and talk like Jesus—to mirror Jesus. You can't do this on your own because Jesus did not do it on His own. Jesus came full of the Word of God—literally, the Word of God made flesh—and then later was filled with the Holy Spirit. He was the fullness of the words of God, and **the Word was the dominant influence in His life**. Jesus operated in the same manner as the Father. He demonstrated love and, as a result, changed the world.

When we get set free from the self-nature, we will faithfully do as Christ did. We will love others even as ourselves. But, if we fail to see that same selfless attitude that Christ had, and still has, operating in our lives today, we must first be encouraged that there is hope and that there is a higher place to which we can aspire.

We must then look to Jesus, allow Him to save us, and ask the same Holy Spirit that He had to come and dwell inside us. This infilling of the Holy Spirit, which we'll discuss in the next chapter, initiates a godly influence in our lives. If we allow the Holy Spirit to be the prevailing influence in our lives, this choice will set us on the road to Christlike living. It is this hope that calls us onward even when we don't see the fullness of Christ's life yet in operation in our own lives. Jesus did it while He was in the flesh, as we are, which means we can do it, too. That divine enablement is why the Spirit of God was sent here. The ball is in your court; what will you do with it?

What is the best way that we can be Christians? Obey. What is the best way that we can obey? Know what He wants you to do. How do we know what He wants us to do? Read His words and submit to the five-fold ministry on earth today: the apostle, prophet, pastor, teacher, and evangelist. Once you are given instructions, follow them.

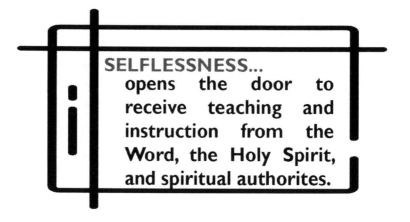

SELFLESSNESS... opens the door to receive teaching and instruction from the Word, the Holy Spirit, and spiritual authorites.

9

Step 2:
Empowerment of
the Spirit

When I was a young man, I was taught that Jesus was perfect and never sinned. I believed that Jesus' ability to live His life above sin was due to the fact that He was and is God's Son. I thought that because Jesus was God manifested in human form, He possessed something that I could not possess. Due to this core belief, I found myself living in sin for much of my adolescent and young adult life. In my mind, I would justify this sinful behavior with thoughts like, *"I'm not Jesus. I'm not God, so I should not resist this temptation to sin because I don't have the ability to say no."* This belief prevented me from allowing Jesus' actions to become my own. I had placed Jesus in such a high and lifted-up place, far above lowly little old me, that I could not even dream of attempting to live without sin.

Now that I am older and a bit wiser, I have come to the realization that, though it is important to revere and respect Jesus for who He is, it is equally important to do as He instructed us to do. He came first to demonstrate a life lived above sin and then to show us how to live our lives above sin.

In Romans 8:29, Paul writes, "For whom He foreknew, He also predestined to be conformed to the image of His Son, that He might be the firstborn among many brethren." In plain English, God foreknew and predestined mankind to become His sons, just as Jesus is His son. Additionally, He wanted each of His sons and daughters to be conformed to the very likeness of Christ. Said another way: it was and is God's desire for His children to become Christ-like! To be Christ-like is to act as Jesus acted, much like the word "Christian," as previously stated. This title was given to early followers of Christ because they resembled Christ in both words and deeds.

In short, Jesus came to earth to live out an example of how we should conduct our lives following God's Word. He became the template for any Christian's day-to-day life. Many have heard about Jesus and are inspired by His actions and words. Unfortunately, scores have attempted to live as Jesus lived by their own abilities and failed. I am one of these people. Under my own power, I fell desperately short of the standard Jesus set. Maybe you have attempted to live your life without sin and have come up short, or possibly you felt like it was an impossible task and decided that you would fail if you tried. Regardless of who you are or what you believe, I have good news for you!

We must first understand that Jesus did have an advantage that some do not possess, yet it is available to every believer. So then, we must pursue and embrace that which Jesus possessed. So what did Jesus have that allowed Him to live above sin?

Jesus' Advantage

Many argue that Jesus was able to live a sinless life and do the miracles He performed because He was the Son of God. That statement is false, and it is particularly dangerous. This statement implies that only Jesus could resist sin's urging or even perform miracles. This line of thinking leads us to believe that we should not attempt to replicate Jesus' works because none of us were conceived miraculously. None of us received the Holy Spirit with physical and audible confirmation as Jesus did. **The true advantage that Jesus had over every other person who came before Him was the empowerment of the Holy Spirit.**

Jesus' advantage was that He was the first human being to "receive the infilling of the Holy Spirit." God's Spirit or presence was reunited with humanity. The Bible says:

> When He had been baptized, Jesus came up immediately from the water; and behold, the heavens were opened to Him, and He saw the Spirit of God descending like a dove and alighting upon him (Matthew 3:16).

Looking back to the beginning of man's time on Earth, we can see where God's original intent was to commune with man—walk with him daily while interacting and spending time with him. All was perfect in the beginning. Man was permitted to spend time with his creator. However, when sin entered the world through "the fall," God cast Adam and Eve out of the garden. Communion or relationship with man changed that day. The ability to be influenced by the Father's presence and to know Him intimately stopped that day.

111

When Jesus received the infilling of the Holy Spirit, it was the first step toward reuniting all of mankind with God's presence. As shown in this light, the infilling of the Holy Spirit should be our highest priority if we truly want to live as Jesus lived.

Intimacy Restored

Another advantage that Jesus enjoyed over others was that He could spend time in God's presence. Prior to coming in human form, the Son dwelled with the Father; He spent time with God and was close to Him. This intimate relationship with God equipped Jesus to facilitate the Father's plans and to carry out His vision for mankind.

When Jesus died for you and me on the cross, He destroyed the barrier preventing intimacy between God and man. Jesus' death destroyed the power of sin and restored to mankind the ability to commune with God by way of the infilling of the Holy Spirit. Jesus said He would send the Holy Spirit, the Spirit of Truth, who would teach and guide us in all truth. Receiving the Holy Spirit into your life opens the door to an intimate relationship with God.

Focus on Proper Influence

Did you know that God's Holy Spirit was sent to Earth to empower you? In place of the word "empower," we could substitute a different word; the Holy Spirit was sent to influence you. The word "influence" is encapsulated in "grace," which unfortunately gets used outside the context and purpose for which the New Testament authors originally selected it.

"Grace" is defined in the **Strong's Concordance** as "the divine influence upon the heart and its reflection in the life." It is the mechanism that empowers us to fulfill God's call on our lives. Accomplishing the call is impossible without the Holy Spirit; the order would be too tall and the task too difficult without Him. But, thanks be to God; nothing is too difficult with Him. Through the Holy Spirit's influence, we are enabled to fulfill the call of God on our lives.

Improper Use of the Word "Grace"

Unfortunately, many Christians today have adopted a belief system around the notion that God's grace is a cover for sin. Therefore, since grace only covers sin, they have no obligation to stop sinning. There seems to be an overwhelming push by those with an improper understanding of grace to promote an ideology that living our lives above sin is impossible. Because of this belief, they are deceived into believing that God's grace will cover each new sin committed without a requirement to repent or change their behavior. Unfortunately, this "greasy grace" mentality has convinced them that sin is a way of life here on Earth and that we should not resist the temptation to sin.

This incorrect ideology is not new. In Jude verses 3 and 4, we can read where this issue was present in the early church. Let's read these two verses from *The Message Bible*, which has a clear depiction of the content written:

> Dear friends, I've dropped everything to write
> you about this life of salvation that we have in

common. I have to write insisting—begging!—
that you fight with everything you have in you
for this faith entrusted to us as a gift to guard
and cherish. What has happened is that some
people have infiltrated our ranks (our Scriptures
warned us this would happen), who beneath
their pious skin are shameless scoundrels. Their
design is to replace the sheer grace of our God
with sheer license—which means doing away
with Jesus Christ, our one and only Master
(Jude 3-4, MSG).

From this verse, we can clearly see that some in the early
church chose to listen to the whispering of the enemy and
began to adopt a doctrine of "grace covers all." After
reading this Scripture, I realized that many believers today
allow themselves to be deceived by the same spirit who
deceived those mentioned in Jude. It is evident that the
Bible has much to say about God's grace giving us the
power to overcome sin, not granting us a license to do so.

I am entirely confident that sin should not be tolerated in
the life of a believer, no matter how foreign the thought of
living a sinless life may be. It is true that no man has lived
without sin, with the exception of Jesus. I acknowledge that
and would never attempt to lead someone in that sort of
thinking. However, I want to clearly state that God's grace
should not be used as a license to continue sinning once we
have been freed from the bondage of sin.

Another Bible example that makes it abundantly clear
where God stands on sin and grace is found in Romans 6:

What then? Shall we sin because we are not under law but under grace? Certainly not! Do you not know that to whom you present yourselves slaves to obey, you are that one's slaves whom you obey, whether of sin leading to death, or of obedience leading to righteousness? But God be thanked that though you were slaves of sin, yet you obeyed from the heart that form of doctrine to which you were delivered. And having been set free from sin, you became slaves of righteousness. I speak in human terms because of the weakness of your flesh. For just as you presented your members as slaves of uncleanness, and of lawlessness leading to more lawlessness, so now present your members as slaves of righteousness for holiness (Romans 6:15-19).

The apostle Paul concisely says that we should never give ear to any teaching or doctrine which allows Christians to continue in sin under the guise of grace. Therefore, supporting a message where this perversion of God's Word was being propagated is unacceptable.

Replicating Jesus' Actions

You may be thinking, *"I've been a believer for a long time and tried to do as Jesus did; it's just too hard."* The truth is, without first coming into possession of what empowered Jesus to live as He lived, you'll continue to struggle. But there is hope. Living up to the standard set by Jesus is possible for anyone that has first been filled by the Spirit of Grace, the empowerment to live above sin. Dr. Robert Gay defines *grace* as "the divine influence upon the heart and its reflection in the life." The same Holy Spirit or Spirit of Grace that dwells inside of Jesus is available for you and me today! Once you have received the infilling of the Holy Spirit, you are then exposed to a much greater influence than that of the enemy.

With the Holy Spirit's prevailing influence, you will begin to see sin's power weaken in your life. What was once difficult to resist will seem less tempting. Over time, you should realize that you have stopped sinning in an area. Then another sin will cease, then another and another and another.

If you continue allowing the Holy Spirit to be the most significant influence in your life, conscious sin can be eliminated. We are to **pursue** a sinless life until we get to heaven, and at that time, we will be perfected; however, while we remain on the earth, we must continue to battle our flesh. Through reliance on Jesus' sacrifice combined with your desire to live a holy life, you will see faith arise and your prayers avail much. All of this is possible if you believe God's Word and put it into action in your life. Listen to the Holy Spirit when He speaks to you; follow the direction and guidance of the leaders that have been placed in your life. This kind of life is "walking in the spirit" and is what Jesus did while He was on the earth.

Sinless Living

My pastor often says, "How many of you have sinned in the last 30 seconds? Now, how many of you have sinned in the last 30 minutes? What about in the last 30 hours?" The point is that if you can go 30 seconds without sinning, you can go longer as you allow the Holy Spirit to become the greatest influence in your life.

Does this mean you will never sin again once you receive the infilling of the Holy Spirit? From my experience, I can say no. I have sinned since receiving the infilling of the Holy Spirit. But I can also tell you that after receiving the Holy Spirit, sin was no longer comfortable for me. I felt conviction when I sinned and knew I had done wrong. Over time, this sense of wrongdoing intensified, and my resolve to stand up to sin grew. With God's help, I believe your situation can be much like this.

Sin does not magically release its hold on you the day you get baptized in the Holy Spirit. The temptation to sin remains because the root of sin, the self-nature or the flesh, is still exposed to the temporary ruler of this world. But, with time, your flesh-nature will weaken, and your ability to stand up to sinful behavior will strengthen. This ability is the endgame for all believers, which is to be conformed to the image of Christ. How do we do that? By acting like Him all the time.

When you sin, and that sin is brought to your attention through the conviction of the Holy Spirit or by spiritual leaders, your spouse, or any other person, you then have the opportunity to stop that sinful behavior and choose not to do it again. This choice encapsulates what it means to **repent:** turning and going in a different direction—not going back.

Some might be thinking, *"Wow, you sure make it sound easy." You may also think, "I tried to stop sinning before, and I could not do it."* I understand that thought process and felt that way until I received the infilling of the Holy Spirit. I tried to stop sinning with my own abilities and fell desperately short of success in my fleshly attempt to do good. Once filled with the Holy Spirit, you will be empowered to live above sin and walk in victory. The sin that plagued you yesterday will no longer be an issue for you today. The more you allow the Holy Spirit to work in your life, the less sin will be an issue for you.

Remember, Jesus said that no one is good but God? That also means that your flesh-nature, while here on this earth and exposed to the influences of this world, will always be in opposition to God. That is the hand that human beings have been dealt. Only God can empower us to live above sin, which is why being filled with the Holy Spirit is so crucial in the life of a believer.

The Law

In the beginning, there was no law. There was no Law of Moses, no Bible—no rules about right and wrong. Then God gave Moses the Ten Commandments and further commanded Moses to write the Levitical law that outlined the ceremonial rituals and procedures that were to be performed by the Israelites during worship. The Bible makes it clear that no man could abide by the Law, so the Law itself caused man to be cursed (Galatians 3). Without the Law, man's sin was without conviction. There would never have been any conviction without first writing that which was unlawful. Sin, as we know it today, was not a sin to those who had no Bible to tell them that their actions were inappropriate.

When the Law was written, there were two portions. The first portion was the Commandments, statutes, and instructions on behavior toward God and man. The second part was the ceremonial rituals that coincided with sacrifices and worship in the tabernacle. Some Christians will say we are no longer under the law but under grace. Some have a distorted view of Romans 6:14, which says, "For sin shall not have dominion over you, for you are not under law but under grace." They presume that none of the Old Testament is relevant and that grace is merely a covering for sin. Let me make this very clear: Romans 6 does not give sin a pass. The truth that we are no longer under the law does not mean that we are no longer required to obey any of the commandments, statutes, and instructions found in the Old Testament. In fact, all of the Commandments are rearticulated in the New Testament, calling us to a higher level of obedience to God's commandments through His grace.

God's Word clearly says He is the same yesterday, today, and forever. This means that when God wrote the Commandments, statutes, and instructions, He meant for them to remain. Otherwise, we could all assume that God lied and that He does change. He would be double-minded if He wrote a law and then revoked it at a later date.

The portion of the Law that is not for the New Covenant believer, the part Paul wrote about in Romans 6, is the ceremonial law. Ceremonial law would have dealt with traditions such as blood offerings and sacrifices. These things were obsolete once Jesus became the fulfillment of those ceremonial rituals, which were instituted as symbols of the Christ to come.

119

Purpose of the Law

God wrote the law so there would be order here on earth. He made you, and He made me. Knowing how we would act toward ourselves and one another, He set laws in place—written laws like the Commandments and unwritten laws like the law of gravity—for us to abide by. We don't get to negotiate God's laws. If you don't abide by the natural law of gravity, there will be consequences for your failure to respect that law. The same is true for spiritual laws.

When God wrote that we should not murder, He knew what He was doing. When God wrote that we should not steal, He knew what He was doing. It is amusing that our culture wants to hang on to the laws they like and agree with, but they want to treat other laws like items on a buffet. For example, our culture says sleeping with someone outside wedlock is acceptable as long as it is consensual. Today's culture is indifferent on whether abortion is murder if the parents feel it is inconvenient to bring the child into the world. It's interesting that people having sex outside of marriage are often the same ones seeking an abortion. This behavior is common today, and it starts with picking and choosing which laws we obey and which ones we ignore.

God wrote all His commandments, statutes, and instructions for our benefit. He did not write them to take away some of our fun. God wrote them because He knew the path to blessing is found in adherence to His instruction; He wants you blessed. What father does not want their children blessed?

The Heart of the Father

I went with my wife and newborn son to the doctor's office one day. Afterward, my wife told me that my son was having some issues with acid reflux and was in pain. I began to feel anguish in my heart for my son physically, and I told my wife, "I hurt when he hurts." I know this must be how the Father feels about each of His children when we are hurting, and like any good Father, He wants to ensure we don't hurt. With this revelation, we can embrace His commandments, statutes, and instructions because we recognize they are for our making and not for our breaking.

God's greatest desire for His creation, for His children, is for us to live our lives in peace and joy. Therefore, God's motivation for writing the laws was from a heart of love toward His people. Each commandment, statute, and directive was written to encourage people to be good to one another and discourage behavior that would lead to destruction.

When reading the Bible, we need to understand that, like our earthly fathers, God loves us with an undying love. As a matter of fact, His love for us is far greater than the love of our natural fathers. When we study His Word with this in mind, we can clearly see the "why" behind the Commandments.

Receiving the Holy Spirit

Apart from salvation, the day I received the Holy Spirit was the single greatest thing that ever happened to me. It was not only a time of joy and exhilaration but also a time of revelation. It was a time when I not only knew in my head that God was real, but now in my heart, I felt He was real. That day, I began to commune with God in an undeniable and personal way that was very different from the day before.

As mentioned earlier, sin created a divide between God and man. When the power of sin was broken, the presence of God was allowed to be experienced by everyone. This is first accomplished by receiving salvation and then asking the Holy Spirit to come and make His residence in our hearts.

The Bible says that none may come to the Father except by Jesus Christ. To be in the presence of the Father, you must first be saved. You must name the name of Jesus and *believe* that He came, died, and rose again on the third day. You must believe that Jesus is alive today and is seated at the right hand of the Father, continually making intercession for you until the time comes when He is sent to this earth again by the Father.

When I say "believe," I am not referring to the mental assent that Jesus came and that He's alive today. I mean that you believe in Him to the degree that you do what He asked you to do. You make Him Master and Lord. He becomes the single most influential voice in your life, and you obey His commandments. That is what it truly means to **believe**.

James, Jesus' brother and disciple, said, "Even the demons believe" (James 2:19). Don't you think these disciples had seen a thing or two in their day? They saw people attempting to live as Christians by their own abilities and thoughts. James, full of discernment, heard people saying that they believed in Jesus, but he confronted them by saying:

> Thus also faith by itself, if it does not have works, is dead. But some will say 'you have faith and I have works.' Show me your faith without your works and I will show you my faith by my works. You believe that there is one God. You do well. Even the demons believe—and tremble! But do you want to know, O foolish man, that faith without works is dead? Was not Abraham our father justified by works when he offered Isaac his son on the altar? Do you see that faith was working together with his works, and by works faith was made perfect? (James 2: 17-20).

We must not get caught up in a fleshly, soulish form of Christianity. Instead, our faith should move us to action. Once we have an active faith in God, we will truly believe and have the green light to receive the Holy Spirit. To receive the Holy Spirit with impact and power, you must first be saved, evidenced by true heart change.

Unfortunately, many have not shared this powerful experience. Sadly, some respond to an altar call in a moment of clarity. They run down the church aisle with tears in their eyes and say a sinner's prayer. Then, they get up, hug people, and leave to go about their normal day-to-day business, returning to the sin from which they just declared themselves free. This behavior does not demonstrate salvation and grace at work within the life of a believer. Instead, returning to sin is the manifestation of someone operating in selfishness.

Selfishness seeks to get for self that which it believes is of value. Self says, *"Eternal hellfire and damnation? No, I think I'll choose Christianity with pearly gates, mansions, and streets of gold."* Then, right after the prayer, self says, *"I did not intend to give up all the other fun stuff. I'll have both."* This mindset of having your sin and having your Jesus is a doctrine of devils, and it will cost you your life if you don't correct it.

True heart repentance comes with a hunger for truth. It comes with a drawing toward the Word. It comes with an expectation that God is real and that He has something ten thousand times better than what we may have experienced in this world up until now. True heart repentance and genuine salvation open the door to receiving the greatest gift any person could ever receive: His Presence and His Spirit.

The Infilling of the Holy Spirit

So how do you receive His Spirit? You say this prayer if you're saved:

> *Heavenly Father, I thank You for sending Jesus to be my salvation. Thank You that I am born again, and You are Master and Lord over my life. Jesus, be my baptizer. Today I receive the Holy Spirit to come and dwell on the inside of me. Holy Spirit,*

thank You for being my comforter and teacher. Fill
me with Your power and grace to live above sin.
Holy Spirit, I receive Your infilling and the gift of
tongues as Your Spirit gives me utterance. Use me
for Your purposes and guide me by Your influence.
I receive You today, in Jesus' mighty name. Amen.

Now that you've said this prayer, be silent for a moment. Wait on the Lord to speak to you. As you begin to hear words in an unknown language with your spiritual ears, say them with your mouth. For some, this may be just as simple as a syllable like *"ba-ba-ba-ba-ba."* For others, it may be more elaborate. From experience, people who receive the infilling of the Holy Spirit are the ones who disconnect their minds and begin to use their faith to grab hold of what the Lord is doing. You will not hear audible words in English or any other language that you recognize. You may or may not feel or sense that the Holy Spirit is moving through you. Simply use your faith to take the first step of opening your mouth and letting Him fill it. This is faith in action.

The next thing you need to do when using your prayer language is to remain focused and engaged. You don't want your mind to wander; be mindful that you are speaking to Almighty God. The Spirit is praying through you, and you are a vessel to see those prayers come about in the earth. When you do this, you will find your faith rising and your spirit strengthened.

Bishop Bill Hamon of Christian International wrote a book entitled **70 Reasons for Speaking in Tongues** (Parsons Publishing House, 2010). I highly recommend you read it for further insight into your prayer language and how to use it effectively. One of Bishop Hamon's teachings that had the most impact on my understanding of tongues was: Using your prayer language or praying in tongues is like turning the handle on a dynamo. When the handle is turned, it is like turning a large generator that produces electricity. Praying in our spirit language is the turning of this spiritual dynamo, which produces power in the spirit— the same power that Jesus possessed when He was here on the earth. Praying in tongues empowers us to do the works that Jesus did, and greater works mentioned in John 14:12.

The Narrow Road

Over the years, I have taught in several Florida prisons, and one thing I always caution the inmates about is the fact that every road has two ditches, one on the left and one on the right. Once in the ditch, it does not matter which side you find yourself. If you're off the road, you're off the road. The narrow path is the road, also called the straight and narrow, and we need to find balance in our lives by seeking to walk the narrow road. Jesus said:

> Enter by the narrow gate; for wide is the gate and broad is the way that leads to destruction and there are many who go in by it. Because narrow is the gate and difficult is the way which leads to life, and there are few who find it (Matthew 7:13-14).

Jesus is saying that you must stay in the middle of the narrow road; you cannot stray to the left or right. The ditch of atheism is wrong, just like the ditch of religiosity. With that said, we must study the Scriptures and learn what they say on the subject of tongues and why we should desire to speak in tongues. We are encouraged not to quench the Holy Spirit. It is our responsibility to ask the Lord to teach and reveal His Word to us.

Paul, who wrote over half of the New Testament, is probably our best example of a man who was filled with the Holy Spirit, apart from Jesus. Paul articulates the importance of speaking in tongues and validates it by doing it often. He also points out that speaking in tongues brings God's power into our lives. Let's read several instances where the Bible encourages speaking in tongues.

Jesus first said in Mark 16:17, "And these signs will follow those who believe: In My name they will cast out demons; they will speak with new tongues..." Jesus was the very Son of God on this earth. To reject a direct order or command from Him would be to reject God Himself. If Jesus said that people who believe in Him would speak with new tongues, then that is precisely what we should do. Otherwise, if we refuse, we must ask if He is truly the Master and Lord in our lives.

In Acts 2:4, we read, "And they were all filled with the Holy Spirit and began to speak with other tongues, as the Spirit gave them utterance." In this passage, we see that they began to speak in tongues when the Holy Spirit came. The Holy Spirit comes, followed by evidence of His coming which is speaking in tongues. The Spirit will not go where He is not welcome and will not force Himself upon you. You must receive Him unashamedly, regardless of what others say or do.

In Acts 19:6, we read, "And when Paul had laid hands on them, the Holy Spirit came upon them, and they spoke with tongues and prophesied." The gifts of the Holy Spirit will start to manifest when you receive Him into your heart and then open your mouth and let Him fill it. Notice that not only tongues begin to come forth, but also prophecy. This is literally the Holy Spirit beginning to move through you, speaking things of which you have no knowledge. But, for the person to whom the prophecy is directed, it makes sense and is good for direction.

In 1 Corinthians, Paul writes:

> Pursue love, and desire spiritual gifts, but especially that you may prophesy. For he who speaks in a tongue does not speak to men but to God, for no one understands Him; however, in the spirit he speaks mysteries. But he who prophesies speaks edification and exhortation and comfort to men. He who speaks in a tongue edifies himself, but he who prophesies edifies the church. I wish you all spoke with tongues, but even more that you prophesied; for he who prophesies is greater than he who speaks with tongues, unless he interprets, that the church may receive edification (1 Corinthians 14:1-5).

Paul is doing a couple of things in this passage. He is validating the existence of tongues but also establishing order at the same time. Notice that Paul does not suggest people run wild speaking in tongues in church just because they can. He suggests that if you speak in tongues for a public impartation to others, there must be an interpretation. It is basic knowledge that if you deliver something to others, be sure they can do something with it. This spiritual activity differs from using your personal prayer language without interpretation, in which you pray in tongues for personal edification. It builds you up. If you don't have an interpretation, you should not attempt to deliver a public message in tongues.

My pastor teaches that prophecy is given in your native tongue and is always rooted in exhortation, edification, and comfort. It could also be explained this way. You love your brother or sister in Christ when you edify and encourage them to come to a higher level. Hatred condemns and calls out the shortcomings. Prophecy calls the person to a higher place.

I want to give a word of caution here. The gifts of the spirit, if not balanced by the Word and subjected to legitimate spiritual authority, can get many believers off the narrow road. While pursuing a more intimate walk with the Lord, some can become unbalanced if they focus on a single aspect of truth. Sadly, this often happens when fixating on pet doctrines. Use good judgment and balance your actions with the Word when you receive the Holy Spirit. Avoid chasing after the signs, but instead, chase after God, and as He said, "These signs will follow [you]" (Mark 16:17).

The Balance Between Tongues and Prophecy

Everything in life must find balance. Too much of a good thing can be a bad thing. In this, we must understand that when we speak in tongues privately, we edify and uplift ourselves. As we pray in the Spirit in our prayer language, the Spirit moves, and things begin to shift in the spirit realm. We do not necessarily discern these things with our natural senses, but it does not change the fact that they are happening. Therefore, we should pray in tongues, and we should do it often.

The flip side of tongues is prophecy. We should desire to prophesy to others. Prophecy's role is to uplift others. Prophecy is edification to others. Prophecy exhorts others. When you edify someone else, you become a servant to that person; you minister to them. You endeavor to lift them, which naturally causes you to be underneath. This is the basic foundational principle upon which this entire book was written. Seek to lift others up through your actions, and when your heavenly Father sees, He will lift you in due season.

Getting Set Free from the Self-Nature

Receiving the infilling of the Holy Spirit literally sets you free from the self-nature. The fact that you have the Holy Spirit living on the inside of you, empowering you to live above sin, is all you need to begin applying the teaching of this book to your life. If Holy Spirit is within you, you have what you need to rise above sin. If you choose to allow the Holy Spirit's influence to be the greatest influence in your life, in time, you will see sin's grasp becoming weaker and weaker. If you stick with it, I believe Jesus' command to go and sin no more can be accomplished.

Heeding the Voice of the Holy Spirit

In the *Walking in the Spirit Survey* earlier in this book, **the second question** is, "Are my current thoughts/actions in alignment with the leading of the Holy Spirit?" So now, let's talk about what you'll likely experience when you hear the voice of the Holy Spirit.

To help you correctly set your expectations, please know that I have never heard Holy Spirit audibly speak, and I don't know anyone who has heard God with their natural ears. A few cases are mentioned in the Bible, but I would emphasize that these cases are rare. Therefore, when you pray to be filled with the Holy Spirit, don't wait to hear an audible voice from heaven. You may be waiting for quite some time if that is your expectation.

It is more common for you to have a sensing or a subtle knowing within your consciousness when the Holy Spirit begins to speak to you. The subtlety of His voice may be a bit difficult to discern at first, but as you spend time in the Word and prayer, both in your native tongue and in your spirit tongue, the voice of the Holy Spirit will become more apparent. Learning this takes time, and it will be your responsibility to spend time with God by reading His Word. Become a student of the Word. Read it with the eyes of faith, seeking to apply every page, every chapter, and every verse. You may need to set yourself up for a new lifestyle of Bible study and prayer. With time, hearing the voice of the Father will become common for you. You just need to have ears to hear—spirit ears.

As you hear from the Holy Spirit, you will always need to weigh what you heard against Scripture. God will not say something to you that conflicts with what He's said in the Bible. Knowing this, you must seek to become a student of the Word to help you discern the voice of the Holy Spirit from other voices.

Once you apply this teaching and hear from the Holy Spirit regularly, you can confidently respond to the questions in the assessment. You will know with certainty if your actions align with Holy Spirit's leading. As you choose to be faithful in heeding the advice or leading of the Holy Spirit, things will go well for you. Being obedient to the voice of the Holy Spirit will ensure that you truly walk in the Spirit all the days of your life.

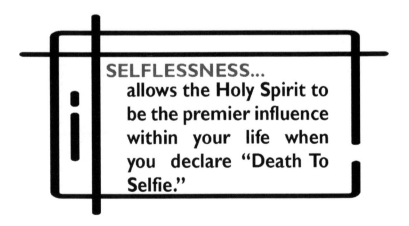

SELFLESSNESS... allows the Holy Spirit to be the premier influence within your life when you declare "Death To Selfie."

10

STEP 3:
SUBMISSION TO
SPIRITUAL AUTHORITY

In this final chapter, let us close with the most practical part of this teaching: submitting to spiritual authority. This chapter will address **the third question** in our *Walking in the Spirit Survey*. Here's a recap of those three questions:

1. Is my current action or thought in alignment with the Word of God?

2. Is my current action or thought in alignment with the leading of the Holy Spirit?

3. Is my current action or thought in alignment with instruction given by spiritual authority?

Applying this survey to major decisions in your life and making a commitment of heart to be faithful and obedient to the counsel you receive will enable you to "walk in the Spirit" all the days of your life.

To balance this teaching, please know that many daily decisions will not require pastoral counseling or ardently seeking the Holy Spirit's guidance. God's not asking you to seek Him concerning the color of your underwear or whether you have white toast or wheat. This teaching requires you to use balance and common sense; it will save your pastor from a phone call or text every other hour. When you have an important decision, and you're not clear whether you're listening to the Holy Spirit or hearing the voice of the enemy, use this guide to help you sort it out. For example, the Spirit will always lead you in a way that regards others; the enemy will always show you a way that considers only yourself. This is how it has been since sin entered the world, and it will continue to be this way until the day the enemy is exiled from the earth. This assessment, or survey, of whether you are walking in the Spirit is the nuts and bolts of living as Jesus did. Jesus lived selflessly.

Let's look at a scenario where a decision must be made, with one choice offered by the Spirit of God and the other by the enemy. You'll find that once you see how easy this is, you will have confidence that you've made the right decision every time.

Scenario: A friend and brother in Christ has fallen into sin. You observe it and are dismayed at the situation but feel that you can do something to help him. After deliberating and praying, you feel led in two directions. In most cases, the first thought is to give advice that puts yourself in a place of being righteous and your friend in a position of error. This thought has the enemy's signature all over it, proudly declaring that "I" have the answer without concern about the advice being received. The second thought on handling this situation comes after prayer and seeking the Lord. In this response, advice is only offered if your brother seeks it from you or has previously permitted you to speak into his life. If so, your guidance must adhere to biblical wisdom and be presented with an attitude seeking to get beneath your friend and call him to a higher place.

Can you see the simplicity of this test? Remember the *Over-Under Hand Drill* that we did in chapter two? Let's do it again. First, place your right hand flat in front of you with your palm to the floor, symbolizing the hand of God. Now take your left hand and place it over your right hand. The left hand represents you, motivated by the influence of the enemy. Satan's signature is always to be over or above the Father or spiritual authority in the earth. Now, take your left hand and move it beneath the right hand. This symbolizes you under the influence of the Holy Spirit and is the signature of Jesus, to come underneath the covering of God and under submission to His spiritual authority.

Every time you do this test, think of your left hand as you and the right hand as your spiritual authority. How do your current actions align you with the hand of God? Are you under, or are you over? If you argue with your spiritual authority, your left hand will be over the right. If you are disobedient to instruction or counsel received by your spiritual authority, your left hand will again be over your right. If you're humble and submitted to what you've been instructed to do, your left hand will be under the right.

If you always seek to place yourself beneath your spiritual covering—God, the Word, Holy Spirit, Jesus, your pastor, etc.—things will always work well for you. You will be blessed in ways you can't imagine. This is what Jesus did, and He is the greatest that ever lived. So, if you want to be great, seek to become selfless just like Him.

DEATH TO SELFIE

Submission to Spiritual Authority

In Chapter 6, we studied Jesus' words and actions concerning submission to the Father. Now, let's discuss how we can replicate Jesus' actions in our own lives. But before we do, let's correctly identify the "Father," who could also be called the "spiritual authority" in our lives. The Father God can be observed working in your life through three different methods:

1. For starters, God's Word, the Bible, should be the first resource we turn to when seeking God's direction in every area of our lives. The Bible was written for our benefit, and we should see every page of it as our connection to Him.

2. Once filled with the Holy Spirit, we should become closely acquainted with His voice, Who will speak if we are willing to listen. The closer you draw to the Lord, the clearer you hear Him when He speaks. Also, I believe it bears mentioning that Holy Spirit will always speak in alignment with the Word of God. We need to understand that God is not schizophrenic; He will not say one thing in His Word and something contrary through the Holy Spirit. If what is believed to be spoken by the Holy Spirit does not line up with Scripture, then you did not hear those words from Holy Spirit.

3. The Father has anointed and appointed men and women to be His hands in the earth, also called the five-fold ministry. This includes apostles,

prophets, evangelists, pastors, and teachers (Ephesians 4:11-12). These men and women of God are placed in leadership positions to perfect the saints for the work of the ministry. To be clear, I am not advocating that spiritual leaders are equal to God; however, God uses men and women in the earth to execute His plans, instruct, lead, correct, and much more. As mentioned earlier, these ministers can be viewed as the fingers of God's hand, doing the work of the Lord. The most common connection you'll see working in your life is likely your local church pastor because the Bible teaches that it is vital to get planted in a local church and submit to the teaching and guidance of your church leadership. Through this relationship, God will do a significant portion of His work if you submit to the process and are teachable.

Advice When Seeking Submission to Spiritual Authority

For those of you who are ready to take this step of submitting to God, submitting to Holy Spirit, and submitting to the voice of spiritual authority, let me offer you some advice. This advice comes to you from a man who has lived this out over the course of fifteen years and is still living it out today.

My pastor once said to me, "Will, not one person has been called into my office for correction and counsel more than you." Then he said, "And no one has taken the instruction and correction as well and has applied it as consistently as you." When I heard this, I thought, "Wow! I am not sure if I should celebrate or be ashamed for putting the man of God through so much grief." After thinking about it more, I looked back at my life up until that point, and I had to admit that I had hurt many people over the years and lived a life full of dysfunction and chaos. But, over time, God has been able to make something out of that mess.

I can tell you that God did not appear in a dream or come out of heaven to give me a vision to bring me great revelation and insight on how to see a change in my life. Here is how it happened: I got saved, attended church for a while, and became hungry for something more. I was filled with the Holy Spirit, evidenced by speaking in tongues. Then, I simply got hold of the Word preached at church, and I got in my Bible and began to read it and apply it. I took it at face value and activated it in my life. I submitted to my pastor and paid attention during service. I chose to listen when corrected, and though it was hard, it was worth it! So here is some advice from a guy that knows a thing or two about this process.

- Find a local church if you don't have one.

- If you have a feeling of peace in your spirit about the church and leadership, become a member.

- Get planted and plugged in; help out in areas where you can lend a hand without any agenda. You are not there to be launched into your own ministry; you are there to serve. If something of value is forged in you, God will call it forth in due season.

- Give of your time and contribute your money through tithes and offerings.

- Once you've developed a relationship with your pastor and determined that this is where God has called you to serve, request a meeting. Let your pastor know you want them to speak—sharing advice and counsel—anytime they see something that needs to be addressed, corrected, or adjusted. Tell them to bring anything that concerns them to your attention at any time. This is submitting to your pastor as a spiritual son or daughter.

- Be willing to be adjusted accordingly.

- Know that it's going to be difficult at times.

- Know that you won't understand much of what is recommended or advised and that it is ok to feel this way.

- Know that whatever you think you will get from submitting to the process and to spiritual authority will not come quickly. It will take a commitment on your part to begin living your life differently than you did before.

- Be willing to open up your heart and let someone else in. Allow yourself to be vulnerable and trust that your pastor will not take advantage of that trust.

- Commit to being at church whenever the doors are open and listen diligently to what is being taught when your pastor speaks.

- If your pastor brings correction or counsel, don't justify your actions. Instead, receive the correction with meekness and humility. Keep your mouth closed and your ears open, committing to refrain from that action with God's help. This is the picture of repentance—turning around and going in a different direction. If an error or problem is discovered in your life, fix it. Stop doing it and turn and go in a different direction. Doing this systematically over a period of time will generate a new creation you won't even recognize in the coming years.

Discerning Wheat from Tares

Many say they want godly counsel, yet often reject it once it's given. This action is not indicative of selflessness or servanthood. Think about this: A master had a servant who worked in his house, and every command he gave was ignored. How long would a servant be permitted to serve if the task or instruction was never carried out? Why do some people think we don't have to listen when our pastor gives us godly and biblical counsel? God put pastors in the church as shepherds to help lead and guide us; this is proper order in the Kingdom. If we can begin to live our lives selflessly— taking the emphasis off our thoughts, plans, ideas, and ministry callings—and get behind our pastor's ministry, we will spiritually align ourselves with what Jesus referred to as "greatness" in the Kingdom. Time spent selflessly living causes us to produce fruit that will be useful to someone else if we choose to serve.

In Joshua Gay's book, **Sonship: The Mantle, The Journey, The Double Portion** (Parsons Publishing House, 2014), he writes:

> The interesting thing about the wheat and the tares is that as they grow; they both look similar. But when wheat bears fruit, it bows itself to the earth, while the tares, who are without fruit, stand straight up. In this, you can see that fruit-bearing creates humility, while failure to bear fruit demonstrates pride.

If you read the story that Jesus tells of the wheat and the tares, the end of the story does not go well for the tares. They are pulled up and cast in the fire because they are useless to the people. However, the wheat produces fruit, which is harvested to bring sustenance and life to those who partake.

As this book concludes, let's consolidate Jesus' words into one simple act. Jesus came to do what His Father wanted, not doing as He wanted. Let's all do the same and see the world change. Let's do what our Father wants and stop trying to do things our own way. Let's get behind our local church bodies and push with all our might to support them. Let's be in church services regularly. Let's intercede for our pastors during our prayer time. Let's give both tithes and offerings. Let's work in the nursery so that someone else can hear the Word preached without a baby crying behind them. Let's help set up for a banquet when asked, even though we're hungry and the buffet is calling. Let's show up when the call is put out for volunteers.

These things are the nuts and bolts of servanthood, and they are the embodiment of selflessness. However, there is much more to this than just these simple actions. As you begin to plug in and get planted, you will start to see the steps to take. You will receive the blessing of wisdom imparted while serving your pastors. In the end, you will be changed if you choose to serve. In this, you will fulfill Paul's instruction to "walk in the Spirit." If you can successfully walk in the Spirit daily, you will fulfill Jesus' instruction to become the least so that greatness may be found in you!

Summary

Death to Selfie grants the reader permission to pursue a life lived above sin. Our goal is to empower and equip believers to say "no" to the enemy's influence and make the Holy Spirit the chief voice within their lives. As we journeyed together, you were taken on a journey of discovering that all sin is rooted in selfishness. Then we did a deep dive into the roots of selfishness, which can always be traced back to the influence of the enemy. Next, we discussed three ways sin manifests in a believer's life. Immediately after, we studied Jesus and His life lived in selflessness. And finally, you were given the tools necessary to implement this teaching in your own life in a practical yet simple way. Ultimately, this author wants you to grow in faith, and as you mature, selfishness is replaced with selflessness—sinful living is exchanged for service toward God and man. If you submit to the process and adhere to these outlined instructions, there is no limit to what God will do in and through you. You will find joy and accomplish every calling and purpose God has for your life.

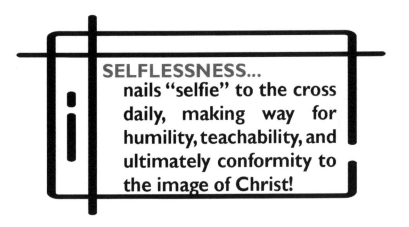

SELFLESSNESS...
nails "selfie" to the cross daily, making way for humility, teachability, and ultimately conformity to the image of Christ!

DEATH TO SELFIE

ABOUT THE AUTHOR

 WILL OWEN is the founder and CEO of JetBoatPilot, a multi-dimensional global company making products for the marine industry. He and his wife Jennifer and their three children, Caleb, Barrett, and Faith, live in Panama City, Florida. Will is an accomplished writer and content creator and is widely acknowledged as a leader and influencer in the Jet Boat segment of the Marine Industry. His work can be found on his company's YouTube Channel, along with numerous other social media platforms. As an inventor, Will holds eight U.S. Patents & Trademarks for products manufactured by JetBoatPilot. He also serves on the Board of Directors for High Praise Worship Center, his home church since 2007. As an engineer and inventor, he brings a unique perspective that helps people find answers to common problems in life. Will's background and business experience enable him to dissect, analyze, and systematically address solutions to common problems we face in our journey to mature as believers. Contact at jetboatpilot.com@gmail.com.

70 REASONS FOR SPEAKING IN TONGUES
DR. BILL HAMON • 9781602730137 • $14.95
Learn how to use your spirit language to activate more faith and increase God's love and power within your life and ministry.

SONSHIP: THE MANTLE. THE JOURNEY. THE DOUBLE PORTION.
JOSHUA GAY • 9781602730526 • $12.95
This journey reveals the principles and praxis of sonship that this generation desperately needs in order to release an empowerment to be world-changers.

NEXT LEVEL: RAISING THE STANDARD OF GRACE
DR. ROBERT GAY • 9781602730427 • $14.95
Using biblical truths, Dr. Gay illuminates the true meaning of grace and its relationship to the Ten Commandments. You are taken on a quest for the grassroots truth that this generation desperately needs for a great awakening.